Nguyễn Thị Tâm
Saigon, 96

Authentic Recipes from
VIETNAM

Recipes by Trieu Thi Choi and Marcel Isaak
Introduction by Annabel Jackson-Doling
Photographs by Heinz von Holzen
Styling by Chistina Ong

PERIPLUS

Published by Periplus Editions, with editorial offices at
130 Joo Seng Road #06-01, Singapore 368357
Tel: (65) 6280-1330; fax (65) 6280-6290
Email: inquiries@periplus.com.sg
Website: www.periplus.com

Hardcover ISBN: 0-7946-0327-0
Paperback ISBN: 0-7946-0328-9
Printed in Singapore

Distributed by
North America, Latin America and Europe
Tuttle Publishing, 364 Innovation Drive
North Clarendon, VT 05759-9436, USA
Tel: (802) 773-8930; fax: (802) 773-6993
Email: info@tuttlepublishing.com

Japan
Tuttle Publishing, Yaekari Building, 3,
5-4-12 Osaki, Shinagawa-Ku, Tokyo 1410032
Tel: (03) 5437-0171; fax: (03) 5437-0755
Email: tuttle-sales@gol.com

Asia Pacific
Berkeley Books Pte Ltd
130 Joo Seng Road #06-01, Singapore 368357
Tel: (65) 6280-1330; fax (65) 6280-6290
Email: inquiries@periplus.com.sg

Photo credits: All food photography by Heinz von
Holzen. Other photos by Doan Duc Minh (page 6);
Hans Kemp (page 4); Tim Hall (page 8); R. Ian Lloyd
(page 15); Luca Tettoni (pages 11); Catherine Karnow
(pages 3, 5, 7, 9, 12, 13). Cover illustration by Nguyen
Thi Tam. Illustration on page 10 courtesy of Léonard
de Silva, Paris.

Contents

Food in Vietnam

One of Asia's best kept culinary secrets—but not any more!

Vietnam is a country on the rise. An almost palpable sense of optimism hangs in the balmy air. The Vietnam War (known here as the "American War") has not been forgotten, nor have the years of oppression and foreign rule, but the country is moving on. The effects of *doi moi*, the economic reform policy allowing small-scale private enterprise, introduced by the communist government in 1986, are becoming more and more evident. The accumulation of personal wealth is now encouraged, joint ventures with overseas companies are welcomed, and many overseas Vietnamese are returning to their country to start businesses after years abroad.

The fancy new restaurants that are restoring life to old colonial buildings, and the modern hotels steadily creeping into the skyline, are just two of the many signs signaling Vietnam's renaissance. And one needn't go farther than a few steps onto any street to experience the thriving culinary scene that is so much a part of this new vitality.

On the streets of Ho Chi Minh City or Hanoi in the early morning, food stalls appear on the sidewalks in front of old shop houses. Clusters of tiny chairs and tables surround a steaming hot cauldron of soup set on an open flame; soon the chairs will be filled with people huddled over their morning bowl of *pho*, a tasty beef broth served with rice noodles and fresh herbs. At another streetside restaurant, a team of female chefs is busy making open-faced omelets in blackened pans over small charcoal grills. Vendors with carts full of baguettes, cheese and sausages are making sandwiches and serving a refreshing beverage of young coconut. Another vendor is wrapping sticky rice in a banana leaf, and handing it to a young schoolboy who is waiting impatiently with his mother.

The markets are a hive of activity as well, literally overflowing with fresh goods trucked in from the nearby villages, the bountiful coastal waters, and the central highlands. Throughout the day, crowds of people fill their baskets from the rows of fresh vegetables and tropical fruits, live fish and game, pickled meats and vegetables, candied fruit, dried and packaged goods, rice and bottles of the pungent *nuoc mam* fish sauce.

There is a renewed vitality in Vietnam that revolves around food. At night, a seemingly endless stream of vehicles parades through the streets. Handsome young men, elegantly dressed women, young couples, and entire families speed about on motorbikes, stopping only to have a beer, talk with friends or have a meal at the literally hundreds of streetside restaurants or at fancy cafés, then race back out to join the nightly procession.

ABOVE: The Vietnamese landscape is noted for its fertility and dramatic changeability.
OPPOSITE: A prime example of one of the many fancy new restaurants, Vietnam House, catering to tourists and returning *Viet Kieu,* or overseas Vietnamese.

A land of breathtaking contrasts

With lengths of unspoiled dramatic coastline, sheltered harbors, fertile and well-irrigated lowlands and vast upland forests, Vietnam is a remarkably beautiful and fertile land, rich in agricultural resources. It is rapidly becoming a major supplier of rice, fish, fresh fruit and vegetables to the rest of Southeast Asia.

Vietnam's narrow curving "S" shape hugs the coast of Indochina for 1,000 miles north to south, and measures just over 30 miles across at its narrowest point. The country boasts a 1,600-mile coastline in addition to countless dikes, canals and waterways, which include the Red River, the Perfume River and the Mekong River—one of the longest rivers in Southeast Asia. It is certainly no surprise then, that seafood and aquatic life are such an integral part of the diet throughout the country.

The other essential component of the Vietnamese diet is rice. The Red River Delta in the north and the Mekong Delta in the south are the two main rice-growing areas, although lush green rice paddies dotted with water buffaloes and rows of women with their distinctive conical hats can be seen throughout the country. The importance of rice to the economy is indicated by Vietnam's ranking as the third largest rice exporter in the world after Thailand and the United States, although the quality of its rice has not been regarded as highly as that of the other nations.

Sixty percent of arable land in Vietnam is given over to rice production, leaving little pasture for cattle farming. Hence beef, in particular, is a luxury for most Vietnamese, and the famous series of dishes, *bo bay mon* (literally, beef done seven ways) is highly regarded. In spite of urbanization and increasingly populated cities, roughly 80 percent of the population relies on rice for its livelihood.

The applications of rice go well beyond simple steaming, occurring in a diverse range of dishes and not always recognizable as rice. In addition to being used in the production of wine and vinegar, rice grains are also converted into flour and used to make rice noodles; rice is transformed into flat rice paper sheets for wrapping *goi cuon*, the Vietnamese fresh spring rolls; glutinous rice cooked overnight, then wrapped into attractive banana leaf parcels, becomes breakfast-time *xoi* or the traditional *banh tay* and *banh chung* eaten during *Tet*, the Vietnamese Lunar New Year holiday (that occurs at the same time as Chinese New Year, and was adopted from the Chinese).

In the cooler northern region (conquered by the Chinese in the second century b.c.), where undulating limestone hills recall Southwest China and where many of the Vietnam's

ethnic groups have their homes, the cuisine shares distinct similarities with Chinese food. Stewing is a popular cooking method, and dishes rated highly in China, such as grilled dog meat and chicken feet are great delicacies. Yet the two most famous dishes from the north are uniquely Vietnamese; both are soups eaten to fight back the winter chill. *Pho* is traditionally a breakfast dish, but can be eaten all day, and

TOP: The quiet journey home from the market.
RIGHT: A bounty of fresh carrots being readied for market in Dalat, in the southern central highlands.
OPPOSITE: Smooth sailing along the tranquil waters of Halong Bay, in northern Vietnam.

6

is as popular in Ho Chi Minh City as in Hanoi; *bun cha* is an aromatic dish of barbecued pork eaten in broth with noodles and herbs.

In the center of the country, which is less agriculturally rich, a lack of variation in the Vietnamese diet and the demands of the reigning emperor spawned a highly developed cuisine. In the imperial city of Hue (the political capital from 1802 to 1945), the symbolic significance of food was refined to a great degree. Small portions in multiple courses, each one more beautiful than the next, elevated the food from common fare to exquisite delicacies fit for the emperor's table. Today, a delicious eggy pancake called *banh khoai* and a soup and noodle dish called *bun bo Hue* are two of Hue's best-loved streetside dishes.

In the temperate south, the cuisine more closely resembles that of neighboring Southeast Asian countries, such as Cambodia, Thailand and Malaysia. The food is more varied and rich than that of Hue or Hanoi, generously spiced with fresh chilies, coconut milk and a variety of herbs and spices.

In Dalat, just a few hours north of Ho Chi Minh City on the southern plateau, the hillsides are terraced with all sorts of western fruits and vegetables—strawberries, artichokes, oranges, mushrooms, carrots, eggplants and lettuces. The abundance of vegetables is so great that many of the region's inhabitants are vegetarians almost without thinking about it. Vast tea and coffee plantations surrounding the area could earn international attention if the quality of the harvest were

improved through better handling and more sophisticated processing methods.

Heavy trucks leave Dalat every morning to deliver a bounty of fresh produce to the burgeoning markets of Ho Chi Minh City. Farther east, down the steep winding road out toward the coastline and the South China Sea, the lowlands are blanketed with canopies of dark purple table grapes. Here several local and foreign companies have joined forces in wine-making ventures.

As investment in agriculture continues to expand throughout the country, the quality of the food produced in Vietnam will certainly improve.

What is Vietnamese Cuisine?

In simple terms, Vietnamese food is lighter and more refreshing than Thai food—using crisp, uncooked vegetables, subtle seasonings, raw herbs, and unique flavor combinations. Often described as textural, with fresh, sharp flavors, it is also more tropical and fragrant than Chinese food.

At the heart of Vietnamese cuisine, with its hearty kick and unique aroma, is the salty, pale brown fermented fish sauce known as *nuoc mam*. The cuisines of Cambodia, Thailand and Burma use a similar sauce, however the Vietnamese variety seems to have a more pungent flavor.

Mandatory in Vietnamese cooking, *nuoc mam* is made by layering fresh anchovies with salt in huge wooden barrels. This process takes about six months and involves pouring

the liquid which drips from the barrel back over the layers of anchovies. The grading of *nuoc mam* is as sophisticated as the grading of fine olive oils. Arguably, the best *nuoc mam* comes from the island of Phu Quoc, close to the Cambodian border. A bowl of steaming rice topped with this fragrant sauce is a culinary treat in itself.

Nuoc mam in its purest form has a strong smell and incredibly salty flavor which renders it an acquired taste for non-Vietnamese. It is certainly stronger than Thai *nam pla* and is used in marinades and sauces, for dressing salads and in cooking. Vietnamese rarely expect a foreigner to enjoy the taste, but are delighted when one does. Easier on the unaccustomed palate is *nuoc mam cham*, which is the ubiquitous dip made of *nuoc mam* diluted with lime juice, vinegar, water, crushed garlic and fresh red chilies. *Nuoc mam cham* is used as a dipping sauce on the table, served with dishes like *cha gio* (spring rolls), or simply as a dip for pieces of fish or meat.

What also sets the cuisine apart from that of other Southeast Asian countries is the pervasive use of fresh leaves and herbs, which come in as many as a dozen different varieties. The use of dill in *cha ca*, Hanoi's famous fish dish served at the popular Cha Ca La Vong restaurant in the city's Old Quarter, and also in fish congee, is likely borrowed from the French, however the extensive use of a variety of raw herbs nevertheless seems uniquely Vietnamese.

While Vietnamese restaurants in other regions of the world rarely manage to offer more than one kind of mint, basil or cilantro, markets throughout Vietnam sell a remarkable variety of herbs. Several varieties of the mint and basil family do not grow outside the country, and there are also some unusual, full-flavored leaves, like the deep-red spicy perilla leaf, *tia to*, and the pungent saw-leaf herb or long coriander that are specific to the cuisine as well.

Every *pho* shop has a huge plate of raw herbs set on each table, and a large plate also appears with an array of dishes, from grilled, marinated beef to *cha dum* (a type of pâté). But what do you do with the herbs? Sometimes, as in the case of *pho*, they are stirred into the steaming soup; with other dishes they are used as wrappers, together with rice papers or lettuces, and are featured in Vietnamese shrimp and chicken salads. The herbs are also served with *ban xeo,* a kind of crêpe enclosing shrimp, pork, mung beans and bean sprouts. Certainly the use of these fresh herbs and leafy green vegetables is part of the appeal of Vietnamese food, providing fresh flavors, beautiful aromas and many interesting textural variations.

Other factors which contribute to the subtlety and uniqueness of Vietnamese food are the refined cooking techniques, the often unusual serving of varying dishes and the combination of flavors.

OPPOSITE: One of the visible signs of French influence is the French baguette. ABOVE: A simple, yet elegant meal in the ancient city of Hue, considered the culinary capital of Vietnam.

The Imperial Cuisine

Hue, situated on the banks of the tranquil Perfume River, is the third most visited Vietnamese city after Saigon and Hanoi. Once an important seat of learning and culture, as well as the imperial seat for nearly 150 years, it is slowly being rediscovered. This rather sleepy place is also the very city which once inspired the creation of most sophisticated Vietnamese cuisine, and took vegetarian cuisine to even greater heights than those reached by masterful Chinese chefs.

Hue traditionally served as a cultural, educational and religious center; it is the site of the country's most important Buddhist monasteries and temples. It was also the political capital of Vietnam, under the thirteen emperors of the Nguyen Dynasty. Major tourist attractions such as the Imperial Palace and the emperors' tombs still suggest a time of great affluence. Emperor Tu Duc (1848–1883), for example, whose expansive tomb reflects his once-opulent lifestyle, is said to have demanded that his morning tea be made only from the drops of water collected by his servants from lotus leaves on the lake within the Imperial City.

Emperor Tu Duc was a notoriously finicky eater, who demanded food that was markedly different from that eaten by commoners. Since Hue lacked the agricultural diversity, the imperial kitchens were required to show an enormous amount of ingenuity—refining ordinary dishes until they became something truly special, so that eating could be viewed as art, ritual and sensory pleasure at the same time. Tea-drinking was also elevated to a ceremony laden with intellectual meaning and aesthetic significance.

A typical imperial banquet today would include a dozen dishes, such as a fragrant, peppery chicken soup with lotus seeds (*sup ga*), crisp, golden brown spring rolls (*nem ran*), delicate rice flour patties stuffed with minced shrimp (*banh Hue*), grilled pork in rice paper (*thit nuong*) served with peanut sauce, delicious crab claws stuffed with pork (*cua phich bot*), and the famous minced shrimp wrapped around sugar cane (*cha tom lui mia*), known in the south as *chao tom*. Main dishes might include fish grilled in banana leaf (*ca nuong la chuoi*), pungent beef in wild betel leaves (*bo la lot*), rice with vegetables (*com Hue*), gently sautéed shrimp with mushrooms (*tom xao hanh nam*), and finally the glutinous rice dessert (*phu the*), literally translates as husband-and-wife cake.

These dishes are actually variations of those served in other parts of Vietnam, and the ingredients may be simple vegetables, eggs or fish, rather than exotic sea delicacies or the best cuts of meat. What sets these dishes apart is the sophisticated cooking techniques and the presentation. For example, the favorite *chao tom* seems so simple you would never guess the complexity of its preparation. The tiny shrimp are carefully shelled before marinating in *nuoc mam*. After washing, they are pounded to a thick paste, and mix with egg white, onion, garlic, sugar and pepper. The mixture is pounded again with a touch of pork fat, and finally wrapped around sugar cane sticks and grilled.

Appearance was very important, not only in the use of color and the arrangement on the plate, but also in the manner of serving. Rice, for example, might have been draped with a generous omelet coat, or cooked inside a lotus leaf and further enhanced with lotus seeds. Chefs also experimented with unusual ingredients such as green banana and unripe figs, banana blossoms and green corn, which until then had been considered unpalatable.

Portions were delicate, with perhaps dozens of dishes served in the course of one meal. Emperor Tu Duc was said to order 50 different dishes every meal, prepared by 50 different cooks and served by 50 different servants. If it was possible to reduce the size of a cake or a bun, it was done. *Banh khoai*, for example, is a smaller version of the *banh xeo* so popular in the south. Even the vegetables mixed with rice are chopped into the smallest pieces possible.

All these requirements naturally increased the length of preparation time, with the result that the number of cooks and kitchen staff reached unprecedented heights—a luxury which perfectly befitted the privileged life of an emperor.

The most talented proponents of imperial cuisine today are virtually all women, each of them descended by some route or other from imperial households. Skills were painstakingly passed down in extended families, with young cooks-to-be encouraged to first observe an experienced cook before being invited to try their hand at actual preparation.

Due to its size and relatively small population, Hue today is not a culinary mecca compared with Ho Chi Minh City or Hanoi. There is, however, a renewed interest in the cuisine of Hue, and a number of modern Vietnamese chefs have made it their mission to turn the simple art of cooking into something extraordinary, and restore imperial cuisine to its former glory.

OPPOSITE: Aristocratic banquets such as this one, illustrated in a French print dating from 1883, were occasions for endless rounds of feasting.
BELOW: The Citadel, or former imperial palace, in Hue.

The Ascending Dragon

Since the mid-1980s, a combination of economic upturn and the return of many overseas Vietnamese (encouraged by the government to start new businesses) has resulted in, among other things, the rebirth of a thriving restaurant scene—from flashy new establishments to informal sidewalk cafés lining the streets.

Culinary skills are being relearned, courses for the training of professional chefs are being launched and, most importantly, the Vietnamese are once again discovering the joys of cooking. Top-quality, fresh ingredients are widely available. Vietnam is fortunate in being able to grow a diverse variety of vegetables and fruits throughout the country. and little food is imported. Rice and seafood are once again in abundant supply.

Restaurants, which reflect this renewed interest in food, are as much about ambience—sipping a *pastis* or lingering over a bottle of fine French wine—as about the quality of food. Found all over Ho Chi Minh City and, to a slightly lesser extent, in Hanoi, these restaurants are often built around courtyards in French colonial buildings or designed to resemble old Vietnamese family homes. With their distinctly nostalgic feel, these new restaurants are not only redefining the Vietnamese aesthetic, but also serving food which is improving by the year. French restaurants are once again establishing themselves, and fashionable Italian restaurants are making an appearance, but the most interesting development is undoubtedly the new Vietnamese restaurants.

Modern Vietnamese cuisine is a marriage of the old and the new. Recipes from past generations coupled with new dishes created for the increasingly sophisticated and well-traveled local consumers. A good example is *thit kho to*, pork cooked slowly in a claypot, a dish of peasant origins which now appears on restaurant menus alongside *cua rang me*, an innovative fried crab dish, richly flavored with tamarind. The traditional Hanoi beef soup, *pho*, served with noodles, bean sprouts and fresh herbs, has gone through many transitions, but remains as tasty today as in the past.

The sometimes lengthy preparation times and cooking processes required by Vietnamese cuisine can render it something of a luxury for people with busy lives, so many chefs and teachers within Vietnam have begun experimenting with new methods that preserve the spirit of the cuisine, but allow it to be prepared quickly and simply at home. For example, deep-fried squid, which is traditionally made with minced squid combined with egg, wrapped in rice paper and then fried, is today being made with whole pieces of squid to save time. The Chinese influence is also being felt. In fact, it is not unusual to find soy sauce on the table alongside *nuoc mam* in the newer restaurants.

Ironically, at the same time that this movement towards quicker cooking has been evolving, there has also been a resurgence of interest in the traditional dishes of the Hue court, the style of Vietnamese cooking that requires the longest preparation time of all. Restaurants specializing in this cuisine often cannot open until after lunch because of the considerable amount of time required to prepare the food, and often close early at night because the food has run out.

More and more attention is being paid to attractive presentation as well, although very few changes, if any, are made to cater to the tourist trade. The changes are subtle and often imperceptible: *ga bop*, a chicken salad flavored with onion, *rau ram* herb and a seasoning of salt, pepper and lime juice, has traditionally been made with chicken skin and bones, but new restaurants are preparing it with lean chicken meat instead. Some fat may also be removed from the meat in the pork and bamboo shoot dish *mang ham chan goi*, a move welcomed as much by health-conscious Vietnamese as by the increasing number of visitors.

The cuisine is based on rice, fish and fresh vegetables. Little oil is used in cooking, except for deep-frying and salads are lightly dressed. Healthy, cleansing soups such as the tasty *canh chua thom ca loc* are featured on menus, fresh fruit and delicious homemade yogurt are often served for dessert, and drinks like freshly squeezed sugar cane juice are widely available. It seems likely that, as more cooks learn how to prepare it, and diners begin to understand and appreciate the flavors, Vietnamese food could become as popular as Chinese and Thai. France, Australia and the United States in particular, are already key centers for Vietnamese food. However, there is nothing like eating at a smart new restaurant in a converted French villa in Ho Chi Minh City.

OPPOSITE: New life is being restored to many elegant French colonial buildings.
BELOW: Saigon's chic new eateries cater to a growing band of discerning diners.

Homestyle Vietnamese Cooking
A personal approach to experiencing the essence of Vietnamese cooking

A soft rain falls as dusk approaches, as so often happens in Vietnam. The suburban streets, lined with houses and gardens, are quiet but for a few workers on their way home. Moving away from the main streets into a maze of alleys designed for motorbikes rather than cars, past the vendor selling baguettes door-to-door from a cart, we reach Tuyen's house. In the large but sparsely decorated living room, Tuyen's husband is watching television with their delightful four-year-old daughter, already in her pajamas, and their brother-in-law from the countryside. He is here visiting his eight-year-old daughter who lives with Tuyen's family in the town of Hue because he, a widower, does not earn enough money to support her. This is not unusual in Vietnam—those with higher incomes take care of those who earn less. It is a happy family scene, and they are all beginning to enjoy the smell of cooking coming from the next room.

Tuyen, slim and elegant, is chopping mushrooms and carrots into tiny cubes on a large wooden board. A talented dressmaker, by day she cuts fabric on the sturdy wooden table which takes up almost the entire room. However, tonight the table is laden with fruit, vegetables, meat and fish fresh from Hue's central market along the side of the river. A pot of gently bubbling water is on a two-ring burner. Tuyen usually cooks in the kitchen under the light of a single bulb, but she does not think that would be appropriate on this occasion.

Tonight she has promised to teach me how to cook Vietnamese food, an arrangement made by my marvelous guide Mai, who is her best friend. I arrive on the back of Mai's 50cc motorbike—a common mode of transportation—followed behind by her niece, a 19-year-old learning English at evening school, in the hope of one day becoming a tour guide. She has been commandeered to help with preparation of a very special dinner, which few would undertake during the week. Tuyen is, I am assured by Mai, the most accomplished home cook in Hue, and even then it takes her a full morning, with two helpers, to prepare a traditionally Hue Sunday lunch.

So what do I learn? I learn that before stuffing a cabbage leaf, it is dipped into boiling water to soften it and remove any bitterness. To soften grated carrot, it is mixed vigorously with salt and then rinsed. To extract the maximum juice from a tiny Vietnamese lime, it is rolled like a piece of dough across a hard surface before squeezing. When boiling king beans, continually remove the foam that forms at the edges of the pan. These are the types of detail Tuyen tells me everyone in Vietnam knows, but it is difficult to believe that there are many people who can carry out these tasks with the dexterity of her slim, strong, and highly competent fingers.

Mai's niece is in charge of preparing the purple banana flower, but through lack of experience cuts it the wrong way. But Tuyen does not panic; she selects some pieces for deep-frying in a wheat flour batter, while the remainder is mixed with just a squeeze of lime and some crushed, roasted peanuts for a wonderfully nutty-tasting salad.

I also learn that tapioca dough is nice to touch, easy to work with, and however much you knead it, it never loses its perfect smoothness—it also takes a long time to prepare. Mai, adamant that she cannot cook, spends almost the entire evening rolling the dough into little balls and stuffing flattened disks (barely larger than a coin) with steamed mung beans seasoned with salt and pepper, or coating roasted peanuts and tiny pieces of coconut in the same dough. The secret is to work with such a thin piece of dough that when each *banh bot loc* (tapioca starch cake) is cooked—about five minutes in boiling water until

LEFT: Although time-consuming, the effort put into the subtle details of food preparation is the key to a rewarding culinary experience.
OPPOSITE: Markets throughout Vietnam sell an extensive variety of fresh herbs and vegetables, which form the basis of the nation's distinctive cuisine.

the pieces float to the top—you achieve a translucence that means you can almost see what is inside. Once cooked, they are immediately plunged into cold water to prevent them from sticking together. We stuff other *banh bot loc* with a single shrimp, a little pork fat and black pepper, this time forming the creations into crescent shapes, then frying them in oil with salt and a little *nuoc mam*.

Tuyen is not only a good cook, she is a good teacher as well. Her four-year-old daughter already knows how to stuff *banh bot loc*, but to play with the peanuts, rather than wrap them, is as much a temptation for this little girl as it would be for a child anywhere.

I learn how to fold rice paper in triangles around a stuffing of carrot, vermicelli noodles, and wood ear mushrooms, with a single shrimp on the top—the tail of which I am to leave sticking out at the top to give this variation on the spring roll the reason for its name, *tom phi tien*, which translates literally as flying shrimp spring roll. Unfortunately, it turns out that I am unable to wrap the rolls to Tuyen's high standards; she is concerned that if she does not re-wrap my efforts, there is a chance that the roll will disintegrate while frying.

Then Tuyan shows me how to make cabbage stuffed with carrot. I mix sugar into the softened, grated carrot, until the sugar has all disappeared, finally adding some crushed garlic. The rolling process using cabbage is marginally easier than using rice paper, but it has to be rolled tight enough so that the rolls can be cut into colorful slices. I find the carrot slightly too sweet for my taste, but am amazed at the firm texture achieved by rolling each leaf so painstakingly tight.

Finally, I have learned how challenging and time-consuming preparing the food can be, the importance of the subtle details, and what a rewarding experience cooking genuine Vietnamese food can be. As we sit down to dine in true Vietnamese family-style and enjoy the rewards of Tuyen's masterful cooking, I discover that eating in Vietnam is a shared experience, an informal ritual. On the small table that the family has gathered around is a large bowl of steaming rice, a cauldron of aromatic soup, and a generous plate of leaves that each of us wrap around a delicious hand roll and dip into the *nuoc mam cham*. Yet, as unique as this experience is to me, I realize that it is simply a typical meal for many Vietnamese families.

Cooking Methods
Tips for preparing traditional Vietnamese dishes in a modern kitchen

Vietnamese food, with its wide variety of textures and tastes, is surprisingly easy to cook. An entire meal can easily be prepared in a single wok or a sauté pan. While preparation has traditionally been complex and time-consuming, modern conveniences such as the food processor make the work faster and easier.

The adage "the fresher the ingredients, the better the food", is especially true of Vietnamese cooking. The various herbs and lettuces are almost always served raw, and salads are never overdressed, so that the full flavors are present. Vegetables and fish in particular, which make up a large part of the Vietnamese diet, are gently cooked and lightly seasoned, allowing the true flavors of the food to come through.

In addition to the ubiquitous and essential **fish sauce** or *nuoc mam* (now available almost everywhere), there are several key ingredients which appear in many of the recipes that require considerable preparation. Ingredients such as garlic, shallots, chili, lemongrass, roasted peanuts and ginger, that have traditionally been prepared with a mortar and pestle, can be easily managed with a food processor or a blender. However, slicing is more effectively achieved with a sharp knife.

Asian **shallots** are deep-fried and used as a garnish. Alternatively, French shallots can be sliced very thinly, sprinkled lightly with salt, then gently presssed with a dry towel to dehydrate before frying (the key to getting them crispy is to remove as much moisture as possible).

MSG (monosodium glutamate) is prevalent in Vietnamese food. However, due to health concerns, we have chosen to omit it from all of the recipes, which may easily be done without affecting the integrity of the dishes. *Nuoc mam*, salt, garlic, pepper, sugar and fried shallots—seasonings used in almost every Vietnamese dish—will compensate for its absence.

When preparing **salads**, make sure that the lettuce is fresh, cleaned and dried (use a salad spinner). Dress the salad shortly before serving, and be careful not to use too much dressing.

Dried rice paper wrappers, used to wrap a variety of rolls, can now be purchased in most Asian food markets. To prepare **fresh rice flour wrappers** (for transparent rolls), most modern cooks will have to improvise by stretching a piece of fine cloth taut over a pot of steaming water. The rice mix (rice flour, water and salt) is spooned over the surface with a large ladle and smoothed into a round pancake. After covering for a few minutes to steam through, it can be lifted up at the edges with a soft-edged utensil,

removed from the cloth, and set aside to be later stuffed, rolled and sliced.

To prepare **dried rice noodles**, use a large stock pot. Fill to a few inches from the top with water, and bring to a boil. Just before the other ingredients are ready, the noodles are placed in a large sieve, submerged in the boiling water until soft, and then added to the recipe.

In general, once the ingredients have been prepared, they should be arranged in bowls or on a large platter, in the order they are called for in the recipe. Then, as you begin cooking, just follow the recipe and the row of pre-arranged ingredients.

The cooking methods most commonly used in Vietnamese kitchens are stir-frying, deep-frying and grilling. **Stir-fry** recipes are cooked in a wok, in either oil or pork fat over a very hot flame, for a short period of time. Sautéing in a large skillet is an alternative method, although not nearly as easy. For those cooks wishing to avoid the use of pork fat (which is difficult to replace), try experimenting with other types of oil. To stir-fry, add the oil to a preheated pan, and follow shortly after with the ingredients that are quickly seared. Cooking generally takes only a few minutes, so that the food does not absorb too much of the oil. A traditional curved spatula or long chopsticks are best for handling the hot food.

To **deep-fry**, you can use the same wok, or a very deep saucepan since a considerable amount of oil is required (peanut oil is preferred). The optimum temperature for deep frying is 375°F to 400°F (190°C to 200°C). To achieve the best results—crisp, not soggy food—cook in small amounts and maintain a high heat but do not allow the oil to smoke.

Grilling is also an important method of Vietnamese cooking that remains as popular and as practical as ever. Using a barbecue is one of the easiest and most effective cooking methods, since grilling over an open flame imparts very distinct and essential flavors that many of the recipes depend upon, although good results can also be achieved using a gas or electric broiler, or toaster oven.

OPPOSITE: Most of the cooking is done over the open hearth in the traditional Vietnamese kitchen.

Authentic Vietnamese Ingredients

Annatto seeds are the dark reddish-brown seeds of the "lipstick plant" and are commonly used as a coloring agent. Usually the seeds are fried in oil to extract their brick red color, then discarded. Commonly available where Caribbean foods are sold.

Asian chives or garlic chives have long, flat green leaves and are smaller than regular chives, resembles flat spring onions. They have a far more emphatic, garlicky flavor than Western chives.

Banana blossoms are the unopened male flowers of the banana plant—a purple-red inflorescence tinged with yellow at the base which hangs at the end of a clump of developing bananas. Tasting like artichokes, the hearts of these flowers, which have been stripped off their purple petals, are a popular salad ingredient in some Southeast Asia cuisines, especially in Vietnam. Fresh, canned and dried banana blossoms can often be found in specialty stores outside Asia, particularly those stocking Vietnamese and Thai ingredients. Choose a firm, large blossom with an even color and check that the outer petals are not wilted. To prepare the blossom for cooking, remove the coarse outer petals to reveal the creamy white heart. Quarter the heart lengthwise with an oiled stainless steel knife to avoid the sticky sap clinging to it. If not cooking immediately, soak in cold water or rub with lemon or lime juice to avoid discoloration. Simmer the cut heart in plenty of lightly salted water until tender, about 15 to 20 minutes. Drain, cool then pull out and discard the hard filaments inside each cluster of yellow stamens as they have an unpleasant texture.

Banana leaves are used to wrap food for steaming or grilling. The moisture and flavor of the banana leaf makes a difference to the texture and flavor of the food, but if you can't find fresh or frozen banana leaf, use aluminium foil. Before using to wrap food, the leaves should be softened for easy folding, either by soaking in hot water for 5 to 10 minutes or briefly heating over a low flame.

Chayote is a type of squash that looks like a light green cucumber, having an oval shape and a small white seed. It is also known as mirliton or christophene. A good substitute is zucchini.

Asian basil   Lemon basil   Holy basil

Basil is often used as a seasoning and garnish in Vietnamese cooking. Several types of basil are used and the most common one is **Asian Basil** (known as *horapa* in Thailand), which is similar to European sweet basil. It is used liberally as a seasoning and sprigs are often added to platters of fresh, raw vegetables. Similar, yet paler in color, and with a distinctive lemony fragrance, **lemon basil** is used in soups and salads. **Holy basil** has distinctive purple-reddish leaves and a mint-like zesty flavor and is used for stir-fries. Lemon basil and holy basil are not widely found outside the region. Basil doesn't store well, so buy it just before you intend to use it. European sweet basil can be used as a substitute for all varieties. Basil has a strong flavor, so don't use more than the repice states.

Dried finger-length red chilies

Fresh finger-length red chilies

Bird's-eye chilies

Chilies have become an essential culinary item in almost every Asian country. Many different varieties are used. The Asian finger-length red chili is moderately hot. **Dried red chilies** of this variety are ground to make chili flakes or ground **red pepper**. Tiny **bird's-eye chilies** are extremely hot. They are also available dried. Whether sliced or minced, the seeds are usually removed.

Coconut cream and Coconut milk are used in many Vietnamese desserts. While freshly pressed milk has more flavor, coconut cream and milk are now widely sold in cans and packets that are quick, convenient and tasty. You should add 1 cup of water to 1 cup of canned or packet coconut cream to obtain **thick coconut milk**, and add 2 cups of water to 1 cup of coconut cream to obtain **thin coconut milk**. If you prefer to use fresh coconuts, you will first need to open the coconut by tapping firmly on the center with the blunt end of a cleaver until a crack appears. Drain the juice and continue tapping until the coconut cracks into two. Place the coconut halves in a moderate oven for 15 to 20 minutes until the flesh shrinks away from the shell. Remove the meat from the shell, use a vegetable peeler to remove the outer brown skin, then grate the flesh using a blender or food processor. Fresh coconut cream is made by grating the flesh of 1 coconut (this will yield about 4 cups of grated coconut flesh), adding $1/2$ cup water, kneading a few times, then straining with your fist, or with a muslin cloth or cheesecloth. This should yield about $1/2$ cup of coconut cream. Thick coconut milk is obtained by the same method, but the water is doubled to 1 cup and it should yield about 1 cup of thick coconut milk. Thin coconut milk is obtained by adding 1 cup of water to the already pressed coconut flesh a second time and straining again, this should yield 1 cup of thin coconut milk. You may also obtain thin coconut milk by diluting thick coconut milk with water.

Coriander leaves or cilantro are the leaves of the coriander plant and are often referred to as Chinese parsley. In Vietnam, coriander leaves are used almost exclusively as a garnish. Fresh coriander leaves should keep for 5 to 6 days in the refrigerator if you wash and dry the leaves thoroughly before placing them in a plastic bag. Italian parsley can be used as a substitute, although the flavor is not at all the same.

Daikon radish or long white radish is a large white radish which can grow to a length of 15 in (40 cm), with a diameter of about 3 in (8 cm). It is normally eaten raw in Southeast Asia, generally after salting to remove some of the bitterness. Choose firm, heavy and unblemished daikons. Pickled daikon radish is yellow or white in color, and sold vacuum-packed and in jars.

Dried lotus seeds are commonly used as the salad ingredient and in desserts. Most lotus seeds are sold with the bitter central core or endosperm already removed (if so, the seeds will have a narrow slit on both sides). Sometimes, there are a few rogues with the cores still intact, so check and if you see a dark greenish center at the top of the seed, split it open and flick out the core. Lotus seeds should be stored in an airtight container in the cupboard; they keep for many months.

Dried rice paper wrappers are wrappers made from a batter of rice flour, water and salt, that are steamed and dried in the sun on bamboo racks, which leaves a crosshatched imprint. Used to wrap a wide variety of spring rolls, dried rice paper wrappers must be moistened before using. Available in many Asian food markets, they will keep for many months if stored in a cool dark place.

Dried shrimp are tiny, orange, saltwater shrimp that have been dried in the sun. They come in different sizes and the really small ones have their heads and shells still attached. Available in Asian markets, they should look orangy-pink and plump; avoid any with a grayish appearance or with an unpleasant smell. Dried shrimp will keep for several months. Before using, dried shrimp need to be soaked in warm water for 5 minutes to soften slightly.

Dried shrimp paste is a dense mixture of fermented, ground shrimp found in the markets throughout Vietnam and other countries in Southeast Asia—sold as solid bricks wrapped in paper or plastic, or crumbled in jars, and ranging from pink to blackish-brown in color. It is used in small amounts, due to its strong flavor, and should be roasted or cooked before using. It may be roasted directly over a low flame using tongs for 30 seconds or heated in a frying-pan, wrapped in aluminium foil for 1 to 2 minutes. Alternatively it can also be microwaved very quickly in a bowl covered with plastic for 30 seconds or so. Do not overcook the shrimp paste or it will scorch, becoming bitter and dried.

Fermented anchovy sauce is a blend of fermented anchovies and salt normally sold in bottles. Readily available in Vietnamese and Thai groceries, this creamy and salty sauce that has a potent fishy flavor is an essential ingredient in Vietnamese Anchovy Dip (*mam nem cham*). Canned fermented anchovies or anchovy paste mixed with a little water may be used as a substitute.

Fish sauce is the ubiquitous Vietnamese condiments used in almost every dish, just as salt or soy sauce are used in other cuisines. Made from salted, fermented fish or shrimp, it has a very pungent, salty flavor in its pure form. Fish sauce is often combined with other ingredients such as sugar, garlic and lime juice to make the various dipping sauces known as *nuoc mam cham*. Use sparingly and always look for a quality brand for a better flavor. Refrigerate after opening.

Five spice powder is a blend of fragrant, sweet spices including cinnamon, star anise, cloves, fennel seeds and Sichuan peppercorns, this reddish-brown powder is popular as a seasoning in Chinese cuisine and some Thai and Vietnamese dishes. Pre-packaged five spice powder is available in Asian markets and well stocked supermarkets. Five spice powder is generally used in small amounts as it is a very strong seasoning. To keep fresh as long as possible, store in the refrigerator.

Galangal is a fragrant root belonging to the ginger family that is used in much the same way as ginger. Known as *kha* in Thailand, *laos* in Indonesia and *lengkuas* in Malaysia and Singapore, it

adds a distinctive fragrance and flavor to many dishes. Though available dried or as a powder, try to purchase the fresh root, which has a richer flavor. Fresh galangal should be peeled before using. The young, pinkish galangal is the most tender and imparts the best flavor. Fresh galangal will keep for several months if stored in an airtight container in the freezer.

Jackfruit s a large, green fruit with a tough, knobbly skin, which reveals a yellow, segmented flesh when opened. It has a taste that is naturally sweet. In Vietnam, the young jackfruit is used like a vegetable in cooking. Readily available fresh in Southeast Asia, the fruit can be purchased canned in the West.

Lemongrass, also known as citronella, is an intensely fragrant stalk used to

impart a lemony flavor. The thick lower part of the stem nearest the roots is the edible portion. Discard the outer leaves until you reach the inner core, which should be moist and tender. When using the stalk, bruise it before cooking and after cooking, remove it from the dish before serving. Lemongrass is readily available fresh or frozen now in most well-stocked supermarkets.

Loofah is a type of gourd with a woody, earthy flavor often used in Vietnamese soups. Any type of squash may be used as a substitute.

Lotus stems

Lotus stems are the graceful stems of the lotus flowers which grow in ponds and dense mud. They are a symbol of purity. The thick roots are used as a vegetable. The seeds are used fresh (for sweet soup or *che*), or dried (in stews). The stems are stir-fried with pork or shrimp, and are also used fresh in salads.

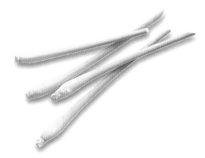

Straw mushrooms   Black Chinese mushrooms (shiitake)

Mushrooms are commonly used as one of the salad ingredients in Vietnamese cuisine, providing texture to dishes. Delicate **straw mushrooms** are the most commonly used fresh variety. Also popular in Vietnam are dried **black Chinese mushrooms** (shiitake). Before using, soak dried black Chinese mushrooms in hot water until soft, 15 minutes to 1 hour depending on the thickness of the cap, then squeeze out the moisture and cut out the hard stems.

Rice stick noodles

Glass noodles

Chinese yellow egg noodles

Bun noodles

Rice vermicelli

Various types of noodles are used in Vietnamese cooking, both fresh and dried. **Glass noodles** or **cellophane noodles** (*mien* in the north and *bun tao* in the south) are dried, translucent noodles made from mung bean starch, which are reconstituted by pouring hot water over them. Fresh, white **rice stick noodles** (*banh pho*) are the wide rice noodles used in Vietnam's classic breakfast dish, *pho*. **Bun noodles** (fresh or dried) are string-like rice noodles that double their size, turning very white when cooked. Fine **rice vermicelli noodles** (*banh hoi*) are similar to *bun* noodles, but thinner. *Mi*, dried or fresh **Chinese yellow egg noodles** are made from wheat and used in soups and stir-fries.

Mint leaves, one of the most common Vietnamese herbs, are indispensable in salads. Mint grown in Southeast Asia has a very intense flavor, the closest equivalent elsewhere being spearmint although regular mint leaves may also be used.

Mustard greens, also known as Chinese mustard cabbage, comes in two basic varieties that are commonly available in Asian markets: one is much more slender and does not form a tightly wrapped head which is usually eaten fresh or occasionally stir-fried or braised, while the other is so bitter that

it is most often salted and sold as a moist pickle known as **Chinese salted mustard greens**. Usually available vacuum-packed, this pickle is used sparingly in soups and some braised or stir-fried dishes.

Palm sugar is a type of sugar made by boiling down the sweet sap harvested from cut flower buds of sugar or coconut palm trees. Palm sugar varies in color, consistency and sweetness from the soft, gooey and creamy beige type which is sold in plastic jars to the crystallized hard and dark brown palm sugar sold in round disks or blocks wrapped in clear plastic or paper wrappers. The dark brown palm sugar is generally sweeter and more fragrant than the others. All can be used. If you cannot find it, substitute dark brown sugar or maple syrup for palm sugar. Hard palm sugar should be shaved or grated into small chunks or melted in the microwave oven to measure before using. Store palm sugar in the same way as normal sugar.

Polygonum or Vietnamese mint (*rau ram*) is an important Vietnamese herb known as *laksa* leaf in Singapore, Malaysia and Australia. It is served with nearly every meal in Vietnam. Highly aromatic, it has a pink stem and pointed, purplish leaves, commonly used as a garnish. A combination of mint and coriander leaves (cilantro) makes a good substitute.

Pomelo, the Vietnamese equivalent of grapefruit, is drier and sweeter, and has a much thicker and tougher rind. It is usually eaten dipped in a chili mix, or crumbled and served in salads. It is increasingly available in the West. Grapefruit may be used as a substitute.

Rice vinegar is mild and faintly fragrant, and is the preferred vinegar throughout Southeast Asia. Inexpensive brands from China are readily available in the West (as well as in Southeast Asia). If buying a Japanese rice vinegar, make sure you do not buy what is labeled "sushi vinegar" as this has sweet rice wine, sugar and salt added. If you cannot obtain rice vinegar, use distilled white vinegar.

Rice wine is fermented from freshly steamed glutinous rice and has a relatively low alcoholic content. Widely used in Asian cooking, rice wine is readily available in bottles in Asian markets. Japanese rice wine or sake and the sweeter *mirin* or sherry may be used as a substitute.

Sago pearls are tiny white balls made from the starch of the sago palm. They soften and turn transparent when cooked, and help thicken coconut milk or water with their gluey texture. Sago pearls are used in Vietnamese desserts. Available in packets in the dry foods section of Asian supermarkets.

Saw-leaf herb which smells like coriander (cilantro), is part of the standard garnish of fresh herbs that are served on the table with most Vietnamese meals. It has a long, serrated green leaf. Also known as "long coriander."

Sesame rice crackers are thin crackers made from rice flour and sesame seeds. They must be grilled or lightly baked before serving and are used like a cracker for dipping. Shrimp crackers or puffed rice crackers may be substituted.

Shrimp crackers, also called shrimp chips, are crispy crackers made from finely ground shrimp, tapioca starch, and egg whites pressed together and dried. When fried in hot oil, they expand into light crackers that dissolve in your mouth, leaving a mild shrimp taste. Very popular in Vietnam, particularly during Tet, they are often served as a snack with a dipping sauce, or as an accompaniment to a main course.

Star anise is a star-shaped, eight-pointed pod from an evergreen tree grown in northern Vietnam. It has the pungent flavor of aniseed or licorice. Used most often in soups (*pho*, in particular) or other recipes requiring long simmering, star anise is available whole or ground. If used whole, discard before serving.

Starfruit is eaten raw and finely sliced. The young starfruit has a tart taste, and is often served with unripe, sliced bananas. Delicious with grilled or fried foods.

Sugar cane is a tall, coarse cane that grows with a thick dense stem and is the primary source of the world's refined white sugar. The sweet juice extracted from fresh sugar cane is a very popular drink in most parts of Southeast Asia. In Vietnam, fresh sugar cane stalks are used as skewers in some dishes, such as the famous *chao tom lui mia*. The fresh, frozen or canned stalks, which look like cane or bamboo, can be purchased in Asian food stores.

Tamarind is a large, brown pod with soft, sour pulp and hard, black seeds. Tamarind pulp is rich in vitamin and has a tangy, acidic taste, and is used as a popular souring agent throughout the world. It can be bought fresh, dried, or in pulp form, and is most commonly sold in compressed blocks, with the seeds removed. To make tamarind juice, mix 1 tablespoon of the dried tamarind pulp with 2 tablespoons of warm water, then mash well and strain to remove the seeds and fibers.

Tapioca starch or tapioca flour is also known as cassava flour. This starch from the cassava root is used as a thickening agent. Combined with rice flour, it adds a translucent sheen and chewiness to pastries. Available in many Asian food markets. Cornstarch may be used as a substitute.

Taro is a starchy tuber that looks like and is used like a potato. It has a brown and hairy outer skin that must first be removed before cooking. Its flesh may be white, pink or purplish inside with the texture of a potato but a unique taste and flavor. It is normally boiled, baked, fried or steamed. There are two kinds of taro—a larger one the size of a baseball and a miniature taro

Firm tofu

Pressed tofu
(*tau kwa* or *tou gan*)

Tofu is a soft, protein-rich food also known as bean curd which is made by curdling fresh soybean milk with a coagulant. It is available in various forms and consistencies, depending on its water content. **Pressed tofu** (*tau kwa* or *tou gan*) has been compressed to remove much of the moisture and forms a dense and solid cake. It is normally deep-fried and holds up well in stir-fried dishes or on the grill. **Firm tofu** is reasonably soft and sold in blocks, immersed in water. It is generally used in soups and braised dishes. Fresh tofu has a very short shelf life. Keep refrigerated immersed in water and changing the water frequently, for up to 2 to 3 days.

for their crunchy texture and to make a fine filling. Fresh or dried wood ear fungus are available. Soak dried wood ear fungus in water until soft before using. Wash well and discard any hard patch that may be growing in the center of the mature fungus.

similar in size to a baby potato. Choose taro that is firm and hairy. It may be stored in a cool and dry place for up to a week.

Turmeric is a bright yellow-orange tuber from the same family as ginger and galangal, with a more subtle flavor. Turmeric is used often in curries and as a coloring agent.

Water spinach is also referred to as morning glory, water convolvulus or *kangkong*. Water spinach, with its arrowhead-shaped leaves and long, hollow stems, has a soft and appealing crunchy texture when cooked. Both the leaves and a portion of the stems are eaten. Young shoots may be eaten raw with a dip. Fresh water spinach is widely available in Asian food stores. Choose

water spinach that looks fresh and has no yellowish leaves. Buy more than you think you need, as it reduces to about a quarter of its fresh volume when cooked. It does not keep well; wrap in damp newspaper or cloth and refrigerate for 1 to 2 days only. If not available, use spinach or bok choy as a substitute.

Wild betel leaves are the spicy and highly nutritious leaves of a vine related to the black pepper plant. In Vietnam, the large, round and crinkled leaf is used as a leafy green in soups, as an outer wrapping for spring rolls and beef, and as part of the standard garnish. Grape leaves are a good substitute.

Wood ear fungus is a favorite ingredient in Vietnamese cuisine. Having very little flavor, they are added to dishes

Authentic Vietnamese Recipes

Preserved Mixed Vegetables
Do Thua

1 tablespoon salt
1 cup (6 oz/175 g) thinly sliced daikon radish
1 cup (4 oz/100 g) thinly sliced carrot
1 cup (5 oz/150 g) thinly sliced chayote (choko) or green papaya
1/2 cup (4 oz/100 g) thinly sliced shallots (about 12 shallots)
1 cup (250 ml) fish sauce
1/4 cup (50 g) shaved palm sugar or dark brown sugar
2 to 3 finger-length red chilies, deseeded and sliced
2 cloves garlic, minced
1 teaspoon salt
1 teaspoon ground white pepper

Rub the salt onto the daikon slices and set aside for 30 minutes, then rinse, drain and pat dry with paper towels. Dry all the vegetables in the sun for a day or in the oven for about 3 hours at 225°F (110°C). Place all the dried vegetables in a sterilized glass jar. Bring the fish sauce, palm sugar, chilies, garlic, salt and pepper to a boil in a saucepan, and simmer for 10 minutes or until the mixture is reduced by one-third. Remove from the heat and set aside to cool. Pour the mixture into the jar containing the dried vegetables and close the lid tightly. Marinate at room temperature for at least 1 week before serving.

Note: When making preserved vegetables, thoroughly clean the glass jar with soap and rinse with plenty of water. Sterilize by boiling the jar in a pot of water for about 10 minutes before using.

Yields 3 cups
Preparation time: 30 mins + 3 hours to 1 day drying
Cooking time: 15 mins

OPPOSITE, TOP: Pickled Shrimp, Mustard Greens and Pig's Ear. OPPOSITE, BOTTOM: Pickled Spring Onions, Water Spinach, Lotus Root, Baby Pickles, and Mixed Vegetables.
LEFT: An assortment of pickles. From left to right: baby cucumbers, shrimp, mixed variety, baby leek tips and pig's ear.

Preserved Mustard Greens
Cai Chua

8 oz (250 g) mustard greens
1 cup (250 ml) water
2 tablespoons sugar
1/2 tablespoon salt

Dry the mustard greens in the sun for half a day, or in the oven for 1 1/2 hours at 225°F (110°C) until semidry. Blanch the dried mustard greens in salted boiling water for about 1 minute. Remove and drain. Slice the mustard greens into short segments or keep them in whole pieces, then place in a sterilized glass jar. In a saucepan, bring the water, sugar and salt to a boil. Remove and set aside to cool. Pour the mixture into the jar, making sure that the mustard greens are fully covered. Marinate at room temperature for at least 1 week or until the stems turn yellow and crispy.

Yields 2 cups
Preparation time: 10 mins + 1 1/2 hours to 1/2 day drying
Cooking time: 3 mins

Pickled Spring Onions
Cu Kieu

1 lb (500 g) spring onions, bottom white bulbs only
2 cups (500 ml) vinegar
1/2 cup (95 g) shaved palm sugar or dark brown sugar
2 tablespoons salt

Dry the spring onions in the sun for half a day, or in the oven at 225°F (110°C) for 1 1/2 hours until semidry, then place in a sterilized glass jar. Bring the vinegar, palm sugar and salt to a boil in a saucepan. Remove and set aside to cool. Pour the mixture into the jar, mak-

ing sure that the spring onions are fully covered. Marinate at room temperature for at least 3 days. Will keep for up to 3 weeks refrigerated.

Yields 3 cups
Preparation time: 5 mins + 1 1/2 hours to 1/2 day drying
Cooking time: 3 mins

Pickled Bean Sprouts   Dua Gia

2 cups (500 ml) cold water
2 tablespoons salt
2 cups (4 oz/100 g) fresh bean sprouts
1 bunch Asian chives, cut into lengths

Mix the water and salt in a bowl. Soak the bean sprouts and chives in the salted water and chill in the refrigerator for 1 day. Drain before serving. If desired, add some grated carrot to this recipe.

Yields 3 cups
Preparation time: 5 mins + 1 day chilling

Carrot and Radish Pickles
Ca Rot

1 tablespoon salt
1 cup (4 oz/100 g) shredded carrot
1 cup (6 oz/175 g) sliced daikon radish
2 tablespoons sugar
1/4 cup (60 ml) white vinegar

Rub the salt onto the carrot and daikon, and set aside for 10 minutes, then rinse and drain. Gently squeeze the vegetables until dry. Combine the dried vegetables, sugar and vinegar in a bowl, and toss to mix well. Allow to marinate for at least 2 hours before serving. This pickles is at its best when served chilled.

Yields 2 cups
Preparation time: 10 mins

Preserved Cabbage

Bap Cai Muoi Xoi

2 cups (8 oz/250 g) very thinly sliced
  cabbage
$1/_2$ tablespoon salt
$1/_2$ in (1 cm) fresh ginger root, peeled
  and crushed
1 cup (250 ml) vinegar
2 teaspoons sugar
1 tablespoon minced polygonum
  leaves (rau ram)

Mix the cabbage with the salt and ginger,
and set aside for 30 minutes, then
squeeze the cabbage until dry (a salad
spinner works well here) and place in
a sterilized glass jar. Combine the vinegar, sugar and polygonum leaves, and
mix well. Pour the mixture into the jar,
making sure that the cabbage is completely covered, and set aside to ferment. Bubbles will appear when the
cabbage begins to ferment 1 day later.
When the liquid in the jar is clear and
the bubbles have disappeared after 3
days, the preserved cabbage is ready
to be eaten.

Yields 3 cups
Preparation time: 15 mins

Fish Sauce Dip

Nuoc Mam Cham

$1/_4$ cup (60 ml) water or fresh
  coconut juice
1 teaspoon rice vinegar
3 teaspoons sugar
1 finger-length red chili, deseeded
  and minced
2 cloves garlic, crushed
1 tablespoon freshly squeezed
  lime juice
2 tablespoons fish sauce

ABOVE: Fish Sauce Dip with grated carrot (top)
and bottled chili sauce (bottom).

Bring the water or coconut juice, vinegar and sugar to a boil in a saucepan.
Remove and set aside to cool. Combine
with the chili, garlic and lime juice, mix
well and stir in the fish sauce. For a variation, add some grated carrot or Carrot
and Radish Pickles (page 25) to the dip.

Yields $1/_2$ cup
Preparation time: 10 mins
Cooking time: 3 mins

Fermented Anchovy Dip

Mam Nem Cham

2 tablespoons fermented anchovy
  sauce or paste
$1/_2$ cup (125 ml) water
2 teaspoons vinegar
2 tablespoons crushed pineapple
1 tablespoon minced lemongrass
1 finger-length red chili, deseeded
  and minced
1 clove garlic, crushed
1 teaspoon sugar
$1/_4$ teaspoon ground white pepper

Combine all the ingredients in a bowl
and mix well.

Yields 1 cup
Preparation time: 15 mins

Yellow Bean Sauce

Nuoc Tuong

$3/_4$ cup (4 oz/120 g) dried yellow soy
  beans, boiled and drained
2 tablespoons thick coconut milk
2 tablespoons ground roasted
  unsalted peanuts
2 teaspoons sugar
3 cloves garlic
1 finger-length red chili, deseeded
2 tablespoons sliced lemongrass
1 cup (125 ml) water
2 tablespoons oil

Grind all the ingredients, except the oil,
in a blender until smooth. Heat the oil
in a skillet over medium heat and stir-fry
the mixture until fragrant, then simmer
for about 2 minutes and remove from
the heat. Store in a sealed jar in the
refrigerator.

Yields 2 cups
Preparation time: 10 mins
Cooking time: 5 mins

Peanut Sauce   Sot Dau Phong

2 teaspoons oil
1 clove garlic, sliced
4 oz (100 g) pork or chicken livers
1 tablespoon sliced red chili
$1/_2$ cup (125 ml) Yellow Bean Sauce
  (previous recipe)
1 stalk lemongrass, thick bottom part
  only, outer layers discarded, inner
  part sliced
$1/_4$ cup (60 ml) thick coconut milk
1 teaspoon sugar
1 teaspoon salt
2 tablespoons tamarind juice (page 22)
1 cup (4 oz/100 g) ground roasted
  unsalted peanuts

Heat the oil in a skillet over medium heat
and stir-fry the garlic until fragrant, 1 to
2 minutes. Add all the other ingredients
and $1/_2$ of the coconut milk and bring
to a boil. Remove from the heat and set
aside to cool. Blend the mixture in a
blender, adding the remaining coconut
milk, until smooth. Transfer to a serving bowl and serve immediately or
store in a sealed jar in the refrigerator.

Yields 2 cups
Preparation time: 20 mins
Cooking time: 5 mins

ABOVE: Peanut Sauce (top) and fish sauce with
garlic and chili (bottom).

Soy Sauce Dip

Nuoc Tuong Toi Ot

$1/_4$ cup (60 ml) soy sauce
1 clove garlic, minced
1 teaspoon sugar
1 teaspoon ground white pepper
1 finger-length red chili, deseeded
  and minced
1 tablespoon crushed roasted unsalted peanuts (optional)
2 tablespoons freshly squeezed
  lime juice

Combine all the ingredients in a bowl and mix well.

Yields 1/2 cup
Preparation time: 10 mins

Tomato Sauce   Sot Ca Chua

1/2 tablespoon oil
2 cloves garlic, minced
1 cup (8 oz/250 g) diced fresh or
  canned tomato
1/2 cup (125 ml) chicken stock or
  fresh coconut juice
1/2 teaspoon sugar
Pinch of salt

Heat the oil in a skillet over medium heat and stir-fry the garlic until golden brown and fragrant, 1 to 2 minutes. Add the tomato and stir-fry for about 5 minutes, adding the stock or coconut juice. Mix well and bring the mixture to a boil. Reduce the heat to low, season with the sugar and salt, and simmer until the sauce is reduced by one-third or until the desired thickness is achieved. Remove from the heat and transfer to a serving bowl.

Yields 1 cup
Preparation time: 10 mins
Cooking time: 15 mins

Sweet and Sour Sauce

Sot Chua Ngot

1 tablespoon oil
3 cloves garlic, minced
2 tablespoons sliced shallot
2 pickled shallots or baby onions, sliced
1 cup (4 oz/100 g) diced carrot
1 cup (4 oz/100 g) diced green bell
  pepper
1 finger-length red chili, deseeded
  and minced
2 tablespoons sugar
1/4 teaspoon salt
1/4 teaspoon ground white pepper
1 teaspoon Tomato Sauce
  (previous recipe) or tomato ketchup
1/4 cup (60 ml) vinegar
1 tablespoon cornstarch (cornflour)
  mixed with 1 teaspoon of water

Heat the oil in a skillet over medium heat and stir-fry the garlic until golden brown and fragrant, 1 to 2 minutes. Add the shallots, carrot, bell pepper and chili, and continue stir-frying for 1

to 2 minutes. Season with the sugar, salt and pepper, followed by the Tomato Sauce and vinegar. Bring the mixture to a boil and thicken with the cornstarch mixture. Reduce the heat to low, simmer for 1 minute and remove from the heat.

Yields 2 cups
Preparation time: 30 mins
Cooking time: 10 mins

Caramel Syrup   Nuoc Mau

1 cup (250 ml) water
1 cup (185 g) shaved palm sugar or
  brown sugar

Bring the water and sugar slowly to a boil over low heat, then simmer, stirring continuously, until the mixture turns dark brown, about 20 minutes. Remove from the heat and dilute with 2 tablespoons of water.

Yields 1 1/4 cups
Cooking time: 20 mins

Salt, Pepper and Lime Mix

Muoi Tieu Chanh

1 teaspoon salt
1 teaspoon ground white pepper
1 tablespoon freshly squeezed
  lime juice

Combine the salt and pepper in a bowl, then add the lime juice and stir well.

Yields 1 tablespoon
Preparation time: 1 min

Chicken Stock   Nuoc Leo Ga

12 cups (3 liters) water
1 fresh chicken (about 3 lbs/1 1/4 kg)
1 tablespoon white peppercorns
1 cup (5 oz/150 g) sliced onion
1 medium carrot, sliced
1 stalk celery, sliced
1/4 teaspoon salt
1/4 teaspoon ground white pepper

Bring all the ingredients to a boil in a stockpot. Reduce the heat to low and simmer for 2 to 3 hours, skimming off the foam and fat that float to the surface, until the stock is reduced to half. Remove from the heat, strain the stock and set aside to cool.

Note: Use the cooked chicken for other recipes such as Pomelo Salad (page 46) and Cabbage Salad with Chicken (page 47).

Yields 6 cups
Preparation time: 10 mins
Cooking time: 2 hours

Beef Stock   Nuoc Leo Bo

16 cups (4 liters) water
4 1/2 lbs (2 kg) beef bones
2 in (5 cm) fresh ginger root, peeled
  and sliced
2 star anise pods
1/4 teaspoon salt
1/4 teaspoon ground white pepper

Bring all the ingredients to a boil in a stockpot. Reduce the heat to low and simmer for 3 hours, skimming off the foam and fat that float to the surface. Remove from the heat, strain the stock and set aside to cool.

Yields 10 cups
Preparation time: 10 mins
Cooking time: 3 hours

Vegetable Stock

Nuoc Leo Rau Cai

16 cups (4 liters) water
1 1/2 cups (5 oz/150 g) sliced carrot
2 cups (8 oz/250 g) sliced cabbage
3 stalks celery, sliced
1 cup (6 oz/175 g) sliced daikon radish
1 tablespoon salt
1 tablespoon ground white pepper

Bring all the ingredients to a boil in a stockpot. Reduce the heat to low and simmer for 1 to 1 1/2 hours, skimming off the foam that floats to the surface, until the stock is reduced to half. Remove from the heat, strain the stock and set aside to cool.

Note: Stocks should be placed in sealed containers and refrigerated, or frozen if they are to be stored for a longer time. Refrigerated stock will last for 1 week.

Yields 8 cups
Preparation time: 15 mins
Cooking time: 1 hour

Pork Rice Paper Rolls Bi Cuon

4 oz (100 g) pork skin (optional)
1 cup (250 ml) water
2 teaspoons brown sugar or shaved palm sugar
1 teaspoon rice vinegar
1 cup (250 ml) fresh coconut juice or water
1 lb (500 g) pork loin
2 tablespoons oil
2 cloves garlic, crushed
1/2 teaspoon salt
1/2 teaspoon ground white pepper
12 dried rice paper wrappers (each 8 in/20 cm in diameter)
1/2 small head butter lettuce, washed and separated
1 cup (40 g) Asian basil leaves
1 cup (40 g) mint leaves
Fish Sauce Dip (page 26), for dipping

1 Roll the pork skin (if using) and tie it with a string. Bring the water to a boil in a saucepan. Add the pork skin and simmer for 8 to 10 minutes over medium heat until cooked. Remove and drain. When cool, thinly slice the pork skin. Combine the pork skin slices with the sugar and vinegar, and mix well. Set aside.
2 Heat the coconut juice or water in a saucepan over low heat. Add the pork and simmer for about 15 minutes until half cooked. Remove and drain.
3 Heat the oil in a wok or skillet over medium heat. Stir-fry the garlic for 1 to 2 minutes until golden brown and fragrant. Add the pork and fry for about 3 minutes until cooked. Remove from the heat. When cool, shred the pork along the grain into thin strips.
4 Combine the pork skin, pork strips, salt and pepper in a bowl and mix well.
5 To make the pork rolls, briefly dip a rice paper wrapper in a bowl of water until soft. Remove and place on a dry surface, smoothing it with your fingers. Place a lettuce leaf onto the wrapper, top with some basil and mint leaves, and 2 heaping tablespoons of the pork mixture. Fold one end of the wrapper over the filling, then fold the sides and roll up tightly, pressing to seal. Cut the pork roll in half and place on a serving platter. Repeat until all the ingredients are used up. Serve the pork rolls with a bowl of Fish Sauce Dip (page 26) on the side.

Serves 4 to 6   Preparation time: 40 mins   Cooking time: 25 mins

Shrimp Rice Paper Rolls Goi Cuon

1/2 cup (125 ml) water
2 teaspoons white vinegar
1 tablespoon rice wine or sherry
1/2 teaspoon salt
1 lb (500 g) fresh medium shrimp
2 tablespoons oil
7 oz (200 g) pork loin (optional)
12 dried rice paper wrappers (each 8 in/20 cm in diameter)
1/2 small head butter lettuce leaves, washed and separated
1 cup (40 g) Asian basil leaves
1 cup (40 g) mint leaves
2 finger-length red chilies, deseeded and thinly sliced
2 cups (100 g) bean sprouts
1 bunch Asian chives, cut into lengths
Peanut Sauce (page 26), for dipping

1 In a saucepan, bring the water, vinegar, rice wine and salt to a boil over medium heat. Add the shrimp and simmer for 1 to 2 minutes until pink or just cooked. Remove the shrimp and reserve the stock. Peel and devein the shrimp, then set aside.
2 If using pork, heat the oil in a wok or skillet over medium heat. Sear the pork for 1 to 2 minutes until lightly browned on all sides. Add the shrimp stock and simmer for about 15 minutes until the pork is tender. Remove from the heat. When cool, thinly slice the pork.
3 Combine the pork slices and shrimp in a bowl and mix well.
4 To make the shrimp rolls, briefly dip a rice paper wrapper in a bowl of water until soft. Remove and place on a dry surface, smoothing it with your fingers. Place a lettuce leaf onto the wrapper and top with some basil, mint, chili, bean sprouts and chive, and 2 heaping tablespoons of the pork-shrimp mixture. Fold one end of the wrapper over the filling, then fold the sides and roll up tightly, pressing to seal. Cut the shrimp roll in half and place on a serving platter. Repeat until all the ingredients are used up.
5 Serve the shrimp rolls with a bowl of Peanut Sauce (page 26) on the side.

Serves 4 to 6   Preparation time: 30 mins   Cooking time: 20 mins

Vietnamese Spring Rolls Cha Gio

These are the classic, deep-fried Vietnamese spring rolls, also referred to as Imperial Rolls.

20 dried rice paper wrappers (each 8 in/20 cm in diameter)
Oil for deep-frying
1 bunch each of several fragrant leaves (a mixture of Asian basil, coriander leaves (cilantro) and mint leaves), to serve
1 small head butter or leafy lettuce leaves, washed and separated, to serve
1 cup (50 g) bean sprouts, to serve
Carrot and Radish Pickles (page 25), to serve (optional)
Fish Sauce Dip (page 26), for dipping

Filling
1 lb (500 g) lean ground pork
7 oz (200 g) fresh shrimp or prawns, peeled, deveined and minced
4 oz (100 g) crabmeat
4 tablespoons minced shallots (about 6 shallots)
3 cloves garlic, minced
2 to 3 dried wood ear fungus, soaked in water until soft, diced
2 oz (50 g) dried glass noodles, soaked in water until soft, drained and cut into thirds
$1/2$ medium carrot, cut into sticks to yield 1 cup
1 egg white (optional)
1 tablespoon ground white pepper
1 teaspoon sugar
$1/2$ teaspoon salt
3 tablespoons fish sauce

1 Make the Filling first by combining all the ingredients in a large bowl and mixing until well blended. Set aside.
2 To make the spring rolls, dip a rice paper wrapper in a bowl of water until soft. Remove and place on a dry surface, smoothing it with your fingers. Place 1 heaping tablespoon of the Filling onto the wrapper. Fold one end of the wrapper over the Filling, then fold the sides and roll up tightly, pressing to seal. Repeat until all the ingredients are used up.
3 Heat the oil in a wok over medium heat until hot. Deep-fry the spring rolls, a few at a time, for about 5 minutes each until golden brown on all sides. Remove with a slotted spoon and drain on paper towels.
4 Place the spring rolls on a serving platter and serve with the fragrant leaves, lettuce, bean sprouts, Carrot and Radish Pickles (page 25) and a bowl of Fish Sauce Dip (page 26) on the side.

Note: Wrap the fragrant leaves and lettuce around the spring rolls before dipping into the sauce and eating them. This is a fun recipe to experiment with. Try using different ingredients such as ground chicken or duck in the Filling.

Serves 6   Preparation time: 1 hour   Cooking time: 20 mins

Grilled Beef Rolls Banh Uot Thit Nuong

1 lb (500 g) beef flank
10 dried rice paper wrappers (each
   8 in/20 cm in diameter) or 5 fresh
   rice flour wrappers (page 34)
1 cup (40 g) mint leaves
1 cup (40 g) Asian basil leaves
1/2 small head butter lettuce, washed
   and separated
1 tablespoon sesame seeds, dry-
   roasted until golden brown
2 bunches coriander leaves (cilantro)

Marinade
1 stalk lemongrass, thick bottom part
   only, outer layers discarded, inner
   part minced
1/2 tablespoon brown sugar or
   shaved palm sugar
1 tablespoon fish sauce

Dipping Sauce
1/2 cup (125 ml) Yellow Bean Sauce
   (page 26)
2 tablespoons bottled sweet chili sauce
1/2 tablespoon ground roasted
   unsalted peanuts

1 Combine the Marinade ingredients in a bowl and mix well. Place the beef in the Marinade, mix until well coated and allow to marinate for at least 10 minutes or longer if possible

2 To make the Dipping Sauce, combine all the ingredients in a serving bowl and mix well. Set aside.

3 Grill the marinated beef on a pan grill or under a preheated broiler for 2 to 3 minutes on each side, until lightly browned on the outside but still rare inside. Remove and set aside to cool, then thinly slice the grilled beef.

4 To make the beef rolls, briefly dip a rice paper wrapper in a bowl of water until soft. Remove and place on a dry surface, smoothing it with your fingers. Place a few slices of beef, some mint, basil and lettuce leaves onto the wrapper. Sprinkle with sesame seeds and top with a few sprigs of coriander leaves (cilantro). Fold one end of the wrapper over the filling and roll up tightly, pressing to seal and leaving the ends open. Repeat until all the ingredients are used up. If using fresh rice flour wrappers, place the filling onto a wrapper and roll up in the same manner.

5 Place the beef rolls on a serving platter and serve with a bowl of Dipping Sauce on the side.

Serves 4   Preparation time: 30 mins + 10 mins to marinate   Cooking time: 10 mins

Hue Spring Rolls Cuon Hue

1 cup (250 ml) water
1/4 teaspoon salt
4 oz (100 g) lean pork
10 fresh medium shrimp (about 8 oz/
   250 g), heads removed
10 dried rice paper wrappers (each
   8 in/20 cm in diameter) or 5 fresh
   rice flour wrappers (page 34)
10 sprigs water spinach (kangkong)
1/2 cup fragrant leaves (a mixture of
   Asian basil, coriander leaves
   (cilantro) and mint leaves)
1 medium sweet potato, peeled,
   steamed and thinly sliced
1 oz (25 g) dried glass noodles,
   soaked in water until soft, drained
   and cut into thirds

Shrimp Paste Dip
2 tablespoons oil
2 cloves garlic, minced
1 tablespoon dried shrimp paste or
   belachan, crumbled
1 small sweet potato, steamed
   and mashed
1 tablespoon sugar

1 Make the Shrimp Paste Dip first by heating the oil in a wok or skillet over medium heat and stir-frying the garlic for 1 to 2 minutes until fragrant and golden brown. Add the shrimp paste, sweet potato and sugar, and stir-fry until well blended, 2 to 3 minutes. Transfer to a serving bowl.

2 Bring the water and salt to a boil in a saucepan or small pot. Poach the pork over medium low heat for about 5 minutes until cooked. Remove and set aside to cool. Cut the pork into thin slices.

3 In the same pot of salted water, poach the shrimp in the same manner for 1 to 2 minutes until pink or just cooked. Remove from the heat and set aside.

4 To make the spring rolls, briefly dip a rice paper wrapper in a bowl of water until soft. Remove and place on a dry surface, smoothing it with your fingers. Place some water spinach, fragrant leaves, sweet potato and glass noodles onto the wrapper. Fold one end of the wrapper over the filling and roll up tightly, pressing to seal and leaving the ends open. Cut the spring roll into 1-in (2 1/2-cm) segments and place them on a serving platter. Repeat until all the ingredients are used up. If using fresh rice flour wrappers, place the filling onto a wrapper and roll up in the same manner.

5 Top each segment with a slice of pork and a shrimp. Serve with a bowl of Shrimp Paste Dip on the side.

Serves 4   Preparation time: 30 mins   Cooking time: 5 mins

Steamed Fresh Rice Flour Rolls   Banh Cuon

This is where a little kitchen ingenuity helps. The making of fresh rice flour wrappers is actually quite simple and fun, once you master the method. This is another variation on the spring roll, using freshly steamed rice flour wrappers.

2 tablespoons Crispy Fried Shallots (page 42), to garnish

Filling
2 tablespoons oil
5 to 6 dried wood ear fungus, soaked in water until soft, sliced to yield about $1/2$ cup
4 tablespoons minced shallots (about 6 shallots)
1 clove garlic, crushed
1 cup (150 g) minced Carrot and Radish Pickles (page 25)
10 oz (300 g) ground pork or shrimp

Dipping Sauce
1 tablespoon sugar
$1/4$ cup (60 ml) water
2 tablespoons fish sauce
1 tablespoon rice wine vinegar
1 tablespoon freshly squeezed lime juice
1 finger-length red chili, deseeded and minced
2 cloves garlic, minced

Fresh Rice Flour Wrappers
1 cup (125 g) rice flour
3 cups (750 ml) water
$1/2$ teaspoon salt

1 Make the Filling first by heating the oil in a wok or skillet over medium heat and stir-frying all the ingredients for about 10 minutes until tender and cooked. Remove and set aside.
2 Combine the Dipping Sauce ingredients in a bowl and mix until the sugar is completely dissolved. Transfer to a serving bowl and set aside.
3 To make the Fresh Rice Flour Wrappers, mix the ingredients well to form a smooth batter. Fill a steamer with water until $2/3$ full and stretch a piece of cheesecloth very tightly over its top, securing it with a string. Bring the water in the steamer to a boil and brush the cheesecloth with a little oil. In a circular motion, spread a small ladleful of the batter onto the cheesecloth, forming a thin, round layer of batter. Cover with a lid and steam the batter until set, 2 to 3 minutes. Remove by carefully lifting the wrapper from the corners with a spatula. Repeat until all the batter is used up.
4 Place a Fresh Rice Flour Wrapper on a smooth surface and top with 1 heaping tablespoon of the Filling. Wrap into a roll by folding one end of the wrapper over the Filling, then folding the sides and rolling up gently, taking care not to break the wrapper. Repeat until all the Filling is used up.
5 Sprinkle the rolls with Crispy Fried Shallots (page 42) and serve with a bowl of Dipping Sauce on the side.

Note: To save time, you may buy the readymade rice paper wrappers instead of making your own for this recipe.

Makes 10 rolls   Preparation time: 30 mins   Cooking time: 20 mins

Shrimp Mousse on a Sugar Cane Skewer   Chao Tom

This is a very important Vietnamese dish, from the imperial capital of Hue. Fresh sticks of sugar cane are used as skewers. The heated cane releases a burst of sweet cane juice when bitten into.

12 fresh medium shrimp (about 10 oz/
   300 g), peeled and deveined
1 teaspoon sugar
1/2 teaspoon salt
1/2 teaspoon ground white pepper
1/4 cup (50 g) ground chicken
3 tablespoons (50 g) fish mousse
1/2 teaspoon cornstarch
2 tablespoons oil
8 fresh or canned sugar cane sticks
   (each 4 in/10 cm in length)
Sweet and Sour Sauce (page 27),
   for dipping

1 Grind the shrimp, sugar, salt and pepper to a paste in a food processor, then combine with the ground chicken, fish mousse and cornstarch in a bowl, and mix until well blended.
2 Lightly grease your hands with a little oil, spoon 3 tablespoons of the shrimp mixture into one hand and wrap it tightly around the middle of a sugar cane stick. Repeat with the remaining shrimp mixture and sugar cane sticks.
3 Grill on a pan grill or under a preheated broiler for 5 to 10 minutes, turning frequently until crispy and slightly browned on all sides. Serve hot with a bowl of Sweet and Sour Sauce (page 27) on the side.

Note: Crabmeat may also be used in place of or in addition to the shrimp. If grilling is not possible, bake in a preheated oven at 375°F (190°C) for about 20 minutes.

Serves 4   Preparation time: 30 mins   Cooking time: 30 mins

Vietnamese Steamed Egg with Pork and Fungus   Thit Chung Trung

This is a hearty, homestyle dish that can be served for breakfast, lunch or dinner.

2 tablespoons oil
3 cloves garlic, minced
6 eggs, beaten
10 oz (300 g) ground pork
2 oz (50 g) dried glass noodles,
   soaked in water until soft, drained
   and cut into short lengths
2 to 3 dried wood ear fungus or
   black Chinese mushrooms, soaked
   in water until soft, sliced into thin
   strips to yield about 1/4 cup
1 teaspoon sugar
1/2 teaspoon salt
1/2 teaspoon ground white pepper
1 spring onion, thinly sliced
2 finger-length red chilies, deseeded
   and sliced
1/4 cup (60 ml) soy sauce

1 Heat the oil in a wok over medium heat. Stir-fry the garlic until golden brown and fragrant, 1 to 2 minutes. Remove from the heat and set aside.
2 Combine the egg, crispy fried garlic, ground pork, glass noodles and fungus in a bowl. Season with the sugar, salt and pepper, and mix until well blended. Transfer to a steaming dish and steam for 10 to 15 minutes until set. Alternatively, place the dish of egg mixture in a large pot and add water into the pot up to half the height of the dish. Cover the pot and steam over high heat for about 30 minutes.
3 Sprinkle the egg with spring onion and serve hot with steamed rice, and sliced chilies with soy sauce.

Serves 4   Preparation time: 10 mins   Cooking time: 15 to 30 mins

Hue Shrimp and Vegetable Pancakes
Banh Khoai

The Vietnamese version of an open-faced omelet or crêpe, this specialty of many streetside restaurants is also called the "Happy Pancake". The Vietnamese name, *khoai*, comes from the type of pan it is cooked in. *Banh xeo* is the large southern version.

1$^1/_4$ cups (150 g) rice flour
1$^1/_4$ cups (310 ml) water
2 eggs, beaten
$^1/_4$ teaspoon salt
1 teaspoon sugar
2 tablespoons oil
$^1/_2$ cup (40 g) straw mushrooms, thinly sliced
8 fresh medium shrimp (about 7 oz/200g), poached for 30 seconds until just cooked, peeled and deveined
5 strips pork or bacon, pan-fried until cooked and thinly sliced
1 cup (50 g) bean sprouts
2 spring onions, sliced
Soy Sauce Dip (page 26), for dipping

1 Mix the rice flour, water, egg, salt and sugar in a bowl until a smooth batter is obtained. Set aside for 10 minutes, then strain to remove any lumps.
2 Heat 1 tablespoon of the oil in a wok or skillet over high heat, turning to grease the side. Add $^1/_2$ cup of the batter and turn the wok or skillet to obtain a thin round layer of batter. Top the batter with some sliced mushrooms, then cover the wok or skillet and pan-fry for about 1 minute, taking care not to scorch the bottom. Remove the cover, add some shrimp, pork slices, bean sprouts and spring onion on top, and continue to pan-fry the pancake until golden brown and crispy, about 2 minutes. Remove from the heat. Pan-fry all the pancakes in the same manner.
3 Serve the pancakes hot with a bowl of Soy Sauce Dip (page 26) on the side and a plate of lettuce leaves and fragrant leaves such as perillas (shiso) and Asian basil.

Note: The pancakes should be pan-fried over very high heat in order to turn out crispy. They should be wafer thin.

Serves 4   Preparation time: 30 mins + overnight soaking   Cooking time: 15 mins

Vietnamese Pork Sausage with Fungus   Cha Luan

Two very different versions of pork sausage found in any Vietnamese charcuterie.

1 lb (500 g) boneless pork leg, skin and fat removed, cut into thin strips
4 oz (100 g) pork fat, diced
5 to 6 dried wood ear fungus, soaked in water until soft, sliced to yield about $1/2$ cup
2 sheets banana leaf (each 10 x 15 in/ 25 x 38 cm), soaked in hot water to soften, for wrapping

Marinade
1 teaspoon sugar
1 teaspoon baking soda
1 tablespoon tapioca flour or cornstarch
$1/2$ teaspoon freshly ground black pepper
3 tablespoons fish sauce
2 cloves garlic, crushed

1 Combine the Marinade ingredients in a large bowl and mix well. Place the pork strips in the Marinade and mix until well coated. Cover the bowl with a cloth and allow to marinate in the refrigerator for at least 6 hours.
2 Grind the pork fat to a paste in a food processor. Transfer to a large bowl and set aside.
3 Grind the pork with the Marinade and fungus to a smooth paste in the food processor. Combine both pork pastes and mix until well blended.
4 Place the 2 sheets of banana leaf on top of each other to form a double layer. Wet your hands and form the pork mixture into a compact roll. Place the pork roll in the middle of the banana leaf and wrap by folding one end of the banana leaf over the pork roll, then folding the sides and rolling up tightly to form a long package. Tie the package securely with string.
5 Place the package in a pot of water and bring to a boil over high heat, then reduce the heat to low and simmer for about 1 hour. Remove and drain.
6 To serve, unwrap the sausage and cut into thin slices. The sausage can be kept refrigerated for up to a week.

Note: You may use aluminium foil in place of the banana leaf.

Serves 6   Preparation time: 45 mins   Cooking time: 1 hour 15 mins

Cured Sour Pork Sausage with Garlic   Nem Chua

1 lb (500 g) pork loin, sliced
1 teaspoon salt
2 teaspoons sugar
$1/4$ cup (60 ml) fish sauce
2 tablespoons oil
4 oz (100 g) pork skin, diced
3 cloves garlic, crushed
$1/2$ cup (100 g) uncooked rice, dry-roasted and ground to a powder
10 sheets banana leaf (each 8 x 8 in/ 20 x 20 cm), soaked in hot water to soften, for wrapping
2 cloves garlic, sliced
1 finger-length red chili, sliced
Pickled Spring Onions (page 25), to serve

1 Grind the pork slices with $1/2$ of the salt, $1/2$ of the sugar and $1/2$ of the fish sauce to a paste in a food processor and set aside.
2 Heat the oil in a wok or skillet over low heat until hot. Stir-fry the pork skin for about 5 minutes until crispy and golden brown. Remove and drain on paper towels.
3 Reheat the oil in the same wok or skillet over medium heat, stir-fry the crushed garlic until fragrant and golden brown, 1 to 2 minutes. Add the remaining salt, sugar and fish sauce, and simmer until the sauce is thick. Remove and set aside to cool.
4 Combine the pork paste, pork skin and ground roasted rice in a bowl. Pour in the sauce and mix until well blended.
5 Wet your hands, spoon $1\frac{1}{2}$ tablespoons of the mixture and shape it into a ball. Place the ball onto a piece of the banana leaf and shape it into a cube by flattening the sides with the back of a wet spoon, then top the cube with a slice of garlic and a slice of chili. Wrap by folding one end of the banana leaf over the filling and rolling it up tightly, then folding both ends inward to form a little square parcel. Tie the parcel securely with string. Repeat until all the mixture is used up.
6 Chill the wrapped sausages in the refrigerator for 2 days. Unwrap and serve with the Pickled Spring Onions (page 25).

Makes 10   Preparation time: 10 mins   Cooking time: 10 mins

Lotus Stem Salad with Shrimp   Goi Ngo Sen

The lotus flower is the symbol of purity. The stems make a delicious salad, as they have a crisp, crunchy texture similar to celery (which may be used as a substitute).

1 cup (250 ml) water
6 fresh medium shrimp (about 5 oz/150 g)
8 oz (250 g) lotus or celery stems, cleaned and cut into lengths
1 tablespoon minced polygonum leaves (*rau ram*)
1¹/₂ tablespoons sugar
1 tablespoon freshly squeezed lime juice
1 teaspoon salt
1 tablespoon crushed roasted unsalted peanuts
Sprigs of coriander leaves (cilantro), to garnish
Shrimp crackers, to serve
Fish Sauce Dip (page 26), for dipping

Crispy Fried Shallots
3 tablespoons oil
4 tablespoons thinly sliced shallots (about 6 shallots)

1 To make the Crispy Fried Shallots, heat the oil in a skillet over low heat until hot. Stir-fry the shallots for 1 to 2 minutes, stirring constantly, until fragrant and transparent. Remove with a slotted spoon and drain on paper towels.
2 In a saucepan, bring the water to a boil over high heat. Poach the shrimp for about 30 seconds until pink and just cooked. Remove and set aside to cool. Peel and devein, then halve each shrimp lengthwise.
3 Combine the lotus stems, polygonum leaves, sugar, lime juice and salt in a large bowl and toss to mix well. Transfer to a serving platter.
4 Arrange the shrimp halves on top of the salad and sprinkle with peanuts and Crispy Fried Shallots. Garnish the salad with coriander leaves (cilantro) and serve with shrimp crackers and a bowl of Fish Sauce Dip (page 26) on the side.

Note: Most Vietnamese salads are quickly and easily assembled once the preparation is done, and often requiring no more than a light toss with a small amount of dressing just before serving. To save time, you can buy the Crispy Fried Shallots. These are available in packets or jars in most Asian food stores.

Serves 4 to 6   Preparation time: 20 mins   Cooking time: 3 mins

Squid Salad Goi Muc

1 lb (500 g) fresh medium squids,
 body sacs only
2 cups (500 ml) water
Ice water, for cooling
2 tablespoons freshly squeezed
 lime juice
4 tablespoons rice wine or sherry
3 cloves garlic, crushed
1 teaspoon sesame oil
1 teaspoon sugar
1 teaspoon crushed black peppercorns
$^1/_2$ stalk celery (80 g), sliced to
 yield $^1/_2$ cup
$^1/_2$ cup (20 g) minced coriander
 leaves (cilantro)
1 finger-length red chili, deseeded
 and minced
$^1/_3$ cup (50 g) Pickled Spring Onions
 (page 25) (optional)
2 tablespoons crushed roasted
 unsalted peanuts
$^1/_4$ cup (60 ml) Fish Sauce Dip
 (page 26)
Rice crackers, to serve

1 Make a lengthwise cut along each body sac. Open and rinse the inside
well. Score the flesh with diagonal criss-cross slits across the surface. This
allows the squid to cook quickly. Slice into bite-sized pieces.
2 Bring the water to a boil in a small pot or saucepan over high heat. Poach
the squid pieces until just cooked, 30 seconds to 1 minute. Remove and
plunge immediately in ice water to cool. Drain and set aside.
3 Mix the cooked squid with all the other ingredients in a large bowl and
toss until well combined. Transfer to a serving platter.
4 Serve the squid salad immediately with rice crackers.

Note: Squid becomes rubbery if overcooked. To achieve a soft and velvety
texture, barely cook the squid and quickly plunge it in ice water. Squid may
be tenderized by soaking it in milk for a day before cooking.

Serves 4   Preparation time: 35 mins   Cooking time: 2 mins

Young Jackfruit Salad Goi Mit Tron

A texturally pleasing recipe that calls for young unripe jackfruit—different from the sweeter, mature fruit. Young jackfruit resembles a vegetable, with a firm texture and a mild flavor. Lily buds or cabbage can be used as a substitute.

1 small young jackfruit (about 8 oz/ 250 g), 1 cup (4 oz/100 g) dried lily buds or 1/4 small head cabbage
2 tablespoons oil
2 cloves garlic, crushed
4 fresh medium shrimp (about 4 oz/ 100 g), peeled and deveined
2 oz (50 g) lean pork, thinly sliced to yield about 1/4 cup
1/2 teaspoon sugar
1/3 teaspoon salt
1/2 teaspoon ground white pepper
1 teaspoon minced polygonum leaves (rau ram)
1 tablespoon sesame seeds, dry-roasted until golden brown
Sesame seed rice crackers, to serve (optional)

1 Peel the jackfruit with an oiled knife and remove all of the thick outer rind, leaving the inner flesh and seeds. Cut the jackfruit into a few large pieces. Boil the jackfruit pieces for about 5 minutes until tender. Remove and set aside to cool, then cut the jackfruit into thin slices. If using lily buds, remove and discard the hard ends and knot each bud in the middle, then blanch in a pot of boiling water for 30 seconds. If using cabbage, cut into thin slices and blanch in the same manner.

2 Heat the oil in a wok or skillet over medium heat and stir-fry the garlic until golden brown and fragrant, 1 to 2 minutes. Add the shrimp and pork slices, and stir-fry until the shrimp turn pink, 2 to 3 minutes. Season with the sugar, salt and pepper, then add the jackfruit slices, lily buds or cabbage slices and mix well. Finally stir in the polygonum leaves and 1/2 of the sesame seeds, and remove from the heat. Transfer to a serving platter.

3 Sprinkle the remaining sesame seeds over the salad and serve hot with sesame seed rice crackers (if using).

Note: This salad is at its best when served slightly warm. Try scooping up the salad with the rice crackers for a unique combination of flavors.

Serves 4   Preparation time: 40 mins   Cooking time: 10 mins

Shrimp and Green Mango Salad

Goi Xoai Xanh Tom Hap

This is essentially a variation on the traditional Vietnamese shrimp salad—using tart, unripe mango instead of lotus root. Green papaya may also be used.

12 fresh medium shrimp (about 10 oz/300 g)
1 small carrot, grated (optional)
1 green mango (about 5 oz/150 g), peeled and pitted, cut into sticks to yield about 1 cup
1 tablespoon minced polygonum leaves (*rau ram*)
$^1/_4$ cup (60 ml) Fish Sauce Dip (page 26)
1 finger-length red chili, deseeded and minced
2 tablespoons Crispy Fried Shallots (page 42)
1 bunch Asian chives, cut into lengths

1 Steam or poach the shrimp for 3 to 5 minutes until pink and just cooked. When cool, peel and devein.
2 Combine the cooked shrimp, carrot (if using), mango, polygonum leaves and Fish Sauce Dip (page 26) in a large bowl and toss to mix well, adjusting the seasoning with more sugar, fish sauce and lime juice if desired. Transfer to a serving platter and sprinkle with chili, Crispy Fried Shallots (page 42) and chives. Serve immediately.

Serves 4   Preparation time: 15 mins   Cooking time: 5 mins

Pomelo Salad   Goi Buoi

This is a relatively new creation, employing the deliciously sweet Vietnamese pomelo, which is similar to grapefruit, but not as sour.

$^1/_2$ cup (2 oz/60 g) cooked crabmeat or crayfish meat
1 small chicken breast (about 4 oz/100 g), poached until cooked, then cubed
$^1/_2$ small carrot, grated to yield $^1/_2$ cup
$^1/_4$ cucumber, thinly sliced to yield $^1/_4$ cup
1 pomelo (about 1$^1/_2$ lbs/800 g) or 2 grapefruits, peeled and crumbled
1 tablespoon minced mint leaves
$^1/_4$ cup (60 ml) Fish Sauce Dip (page 26)
2 tablespoons crushed roasted unsalted peanuts
1 tablespoon minced coriander leaves (cilantro)
1 tablespoon Crispy Fried Shallots (page 42)

1 Combine the crabmeat or crayfish meat, chicken, carrot, cucumber, pomelo, mint leaves and Fish Sauce Dip (page 26) in a large bowl and toss to mix well. Transfer to a serving platter and sprinkle with peanuts, coriander leaves (cilantro) and Crispy Fried Shallots (page 42).
2 Serve chilled.

Note: Since fish sauce has such a strong flavor, it is always a good idea to adjust the amounts used to suit the dish and your personal preference.

Serves 4 to 6   Preparation time: 1 hour

Cabbage Salad with Chicken   Goi Ga Bap Cai

This is the classic chicken salad dish found in most restaurants throughout Vietnam. The unique combination of textures and flavors makes for a delightful, refreshing treat.

1 skinless chicken breast (about
    4 oz/100 g), steamed or poached
    until cooked and shredded to yield
    about 1 cup
1/2 head cabbage (about 8 oz /250 g),
    leaves washed, rolled up and thin-
    ly sliced
2 tablespoons minced mint leaves
2 tablespoons minced polygonum
    leaves (*rau ram*) or *laksa* leaves
3 tablespoons fish sauce
1 1/2 tablespoons sugar
2 tablespoons freshly squeezed
    lime juice
1/2 teaspoon crushed black pepper-
    corns
2 tablespoons Crispy Fried Shallots
    (page 42)
2 tablespoons crushed roasted
    unsalted peanuts
1 finger-length red chili, deseeded
    and thinly sliced lengthwise

1 Combine the chicken, cabbage, mint leaves, fish sauce, sugar, lime juice and pepper in a large bowl and toss to mix well, adjusting the seasoning with more fish sauce, sugar and lime juice as needed. Transfer to a serving platter and top with Crispy Fried Shallots (page 42) and peanuts.
2 Garnish with red chili and serve immediately.

Note: As with most salads, the cabbage leaves should be rinsed and spun dry before slicing. A salad spinner is an easy and effective way to remove the excess water.

Serves 4   Preparation time: 30 mins

Braised Mushrooms with Soy Sauce   Nam Xao Nuoc Tuong

A simple way of preparing mushrooms, in a sweet soy gravy.

1 tablespoon oil
2 cloves garlic, crushed
1 can straw mushrooms, rinsed
    and drained
1 teaspoon sugar
2 tablespoons soy sauce
1/4 teaspoon ground white pepper
1/4 cup (60 ml) water
1/2 teaspoon crushed black pepper-
    corns
Sprigs of coriander leaves (cilantro),
    to garnish

1 Heat the oil in a wok or skillet over medium heat. Stir-fry the garlic until fragrant and golden brown, about 1 to 2 minutes. Add the mushrooms and season with the sugar, soy sauce and pepper. Add the water and simmer for about 3 minutes. Remove from the heat and transfer to a serving bowl.
2 Sprinkle the braised mushrooms with black pepper and garnish with coriander leaves (cilantro). Serve immediately.

Note: Any variety of large mushrooms will work well in this recipe, and different types can be mixed together for a variety.

Serves 4   Preparation time: 5 mins   Cooking time: 7 mins

Beef and Pork Leg Soup   Bun Bo Gio Heo

Soups are an important part of the Vietnamese diet, often featured as a hearty main course or served in combination with a series of other dishes.

8 cups (2 liters) water, with 1 teaspoon salt added
1 lb (500 g) beef brisket
7 oz (200 g) boneless pork leg, cubed
1 stalk lemongrass, thick bottom part only, outer layers discarded, inner part bruised
$1/_2$ tablespoon dried shrimp paste or *belachan*, crumbled
1 teaspoon salt
1 teaspoon ground white pepper
2 tablespoons oil
1 tablespoon annatto seeds
$1/_2$ cup (4 oz/100 g) thinly sliced shallots (about 12 shallots)
1 stalk lemongrass, thick bottom part only, outer layers discarded, inner part minced
2 finger-length red chilies, deseeded and minced
4 tablespoons minced saw-leaf herb leaves (*ngo gai*)
8 oz (250 g) dried string-like rice noodles (*bun*)
$1/_2$ cup (70 g) minced banana blossom (page 18)
2 spring onions, sliced, to garnish
Sprigs of coriander leaves (cilantro), to garnish
$1/_2$ cup (25 g) bean sprouts, to serve
4 tablespoons minced mint leaves, to serve
Lime wedges, to serve

1 In a stockpot, bring the salted water to a boil over high heat. Add the beef, pork and lemongrass. Reduce heat to medium and simmer half covered for about $1^1/_2$ hours or until the meat is tender. Remove and discard the lemongrass. Remove the beef and set aside to cool. Season the stock with the shrimp paste, salt and pepper and continue to simmer over very low heat.
2 When the beef is cool enough to handle, cut into cubes and set aside.
3 Heat the oil in a wok or skillet over medium heat. Stir-fry the annatto seeds until the oil turns reddish. Remove from the heat, strain the oil and discard the seeds. Reheat the oil over medium heat and stir-fry the shallots until fragrant and transparent, 1 to 2 minutes. Add the lemongrass and $1/_2$ of the chilies, and continue to stir-fry for 1 to 2 more minutes, then remove from the heat. Add the mixture and 3 tablespoons of the saw-leaf herb leaves to the hot soup and stir to mix well.
4 Bring a separate pot of water to a boil. Boil the rice noodles until soft, 5 to 7 minutes or longer as needed. Remove and rinse with cold water, then drain. Transfer the noodles to individual serving bowls and top with the beef cubes, the remaining saw-leaf herb leaves and minced banana blossom. Pour the hot soup into each bowl, garnish with spring onion and coriander leaves (cilantro), and serve hot with bean sprouts, mint leaves, the remaining chili and lime wedges.

Note: Soup can be served throughout the day or frozen and stored for use at another time, so recipes often call for large amounts of ingredients to make a large portion of soup at one time.

Serves 6   Preparation time: 30 mins   Cooking time: 1 hour 45 mins

Hanoi Chicken Noodle Soup Bun Thang

This is one of the many warming winter soups that has been popularized in Hanoi, and is now commonplace throughout the country.

1 fresh chicken (about 3 lbs/1¼ kg)
½ cup (60 g) dried shrimp, rinsed and drained
1 lb (500 g) pork ribs, cut into large pieces
12 cups (3 liters) water, with 1 teaspoon salt added
1 teaspoon sugar
2 tablespoons fish sauce
1 teaspoon ground white pepper
½ cup (4 oz/100g) diced shallots (about 12 shallots)
4 baby leeks or spring onions, sliced
1 medium onion, sliced
8 oz (250 g) dried string-like rice noodles (*bun*)
1 egg, beaten and pan-fried, cut into strips
4 tablespoons Crispy Fried Shallots (page 42)
10 oz (300 g) Vietnamese Pork Sausage (page 40), cut into thin strips
Ground white pepper
1 spring onion, sliced, to garnish
Sprigs of coriander leaves (cilantro), to garnish
Yellow Bean Sauce (page 26), to serve

Accompaniments
1 lemon or lime, sliced
2 finger-length red chilies, deseeded and sliced
2 cups (100 g) bean sprouts, blanched until cooked
2 spring onions, green part sliced lengthwise into thin strands
½ cup (70 g) sliced banana blossom (page 18)
Sprigs of Asian basil leaves

1 In a stockpot, boil the chicken, dried shrimp and pork ribs in the salted water for about 20 minutes, skimming off any foam that floats to the surface. Reduce the heat to medium, season with the sugar, fish sauce and pepper, and simmer covered for about 45 minutes, until the chicken is cooked. Remove the chicken from the stock and set aside to cool. Add the shallots, baby leeks or spring onions and onion to the stock, and mix well. Simmer for another 20 minutes, adjusting the seasoning with more sugar or fish sauce if desired. Keep the soup hot over very low heat.
2 When the chicken is cool enough to handle, shred into thin strips along the grain. Set aside.
3 Bring a separate pot of water to a boil. Add the rice noodles and boil until soft, 5 to 7 minutes or longer as needed. Remove and rinse with cold water, then drain. Transfer to individual serving bowls and top with the egg, chicken strips, sausage and Crispy Fried Shallots (page 42). Pour the hot soup into each bowl, sprinkle with pepper and garnish with spring onion and coriander leaves (cilantro). Serve hot with the Accompaniments and Yellow Bean Sauce.

Serves 8 to 10   Preparation time: 40 mins   Cooking time: 1 hour 25 mins

Beef Noodle Soup Pho Bo

You'll find this soup literally everywhere in Vietnam—from street stalls to fancy restaurants and it is now served in restaurants all over the world. It is practically Vietnam's national dish—the classic breakfast meal, but just as delicious served any time of day or night.

1 whole fresh ginger root (about 6 in/15 cm), rinsed and bruised
1 large onion, peeled and bruised
10 cups (2¹/₂ liters) water
2 lbs (1 kg) beef bones
1 lb (500 g) beef brisket
1 teaspoon salt
3 star anise pods
1 cinnamon stick (3 in/8 cm)
1 tablespoon fish sauce
1 teaspoon sugar
1 teaspoon salt
1 teaspoon ground white pepper
8 oz (250 g) dried string-like rice noodles (bun)
1 cup (50 g) bean sprouts, tops and tails removed
1 medium onion, sliced
8 oz (250 g) raw beef sirloin, thinly sliced
Ground white pepper
1 spring onion, sliced, to garnish
¹/₂ cup (20 g) minced saw-leaf herb leaves (ngo gai), to garnish
Bottled chili sauce, to serve
Yellow Bean Sauce (page 26), to serve

Accompaniments
2 finger-length red chilies, deseeded and sliced
2 limes, cut into wedges
Sprigs of saw-leaf herb leaves (ngo gai)
Sprigs of mint leaves
Sprigs of coriander leaves (cilantro)

1 Grill the ginger and onion under the broiler, turning several times or in a skillet until slightly burnt on all sides, about 5 minutes (see note). Remove and set aside.
2 In a pot, bring the water, beef bones and brisket to a boil, skimming off any foam that floats to the surface. Add the grilled ginger and onion, followed by the salt, star anise and cinnamon. Reduce heat to medium and simmer for about 1 hour until the beef is tender. Remove from the heat.
3 Remove the beef from the stock. Slice the beef into thin slices and set aside. Strain the stock and return the clear soup to the pot. Season with the fish sauce, sugar, salt and pepper, and keep the soup hot over very low heat.
4 Bring a separate pot of water to a boil. Add the rice noodles and boil until soft, 5 to 7 minutes or longer as needed. Remove and rinse with cold water, then drain.
5 Place the rice noodles into individual serving bowls and top with the bean sprouts, onion, cooked and raw beef slices. Pour the hot soup into each bowl (the raw beef will partially cook in the boiling soup), sprinkle with pepper and garnish with spring onion and saw-leaf herb leaves.
6 Serve hot with the Accompaniments, and bowls of chili sauce and Yellow Bean Sauce (page 26) on the side.

Note: The ginger and onion can be grilled either under the broiler or simply dry-roasted in a skillet until slightly burnt. Chicken is a delicious alternative to beef, and most Vietnamese restaurants offer both versions.

Serves 4 to 6   Preparation time: 30 mins   Cooking time: 1 hour 15 mins

Crab Soup with Tofu and Rice Noodles
Bun Rieu

2 lbs (1 kg) fresh medium crabs
6 cups (1$^1/_2$ liters) water
$^1/_2$ teaspoon sugar
$^1/_2$ teaspoon dried shrimp paste *belachan*, crumbled
$^1/_2$ teaspoon salt
2 tablespoons oil
1 cake pressed tofu (about 7 oz/200 g), cubed
3 cloves garlic, crushed
2 tablespoons thinly sliced baby leeks
1 large tomato, cut in wedges
2 tablespoons fish sauce
2 tablespoons tamarind juice (page 22)
8 oz (250 g) dried string-like rice noodles (*bun*) or rice vermicelli
1 spring onion, sliced, to garnish
Sprigs of coriander leaves (cilantro), to garnish

Accompaniments
1 finger-length red chili, deseeded and thinly sliced
$^1/_2$ cup (25 g) bean sprouts
$^1/_2$ cup (20 g) minced coriander leaves (cilantro)
$^1/_2$ cup (20 g) mint leaves
$^1/_2$ cup (30 g) sliced water spinach (*kangkong*)
$^1/_2$ cup (20 g) sliced saw-leaf herb leaves (*ngo gai*)
$^1/_2$ cup (70 g) sliced banana blossom (page 18) or cabbage
1 lime, sliced

1 Scrub and rinse the crabs thoroughly. Detach the claws from each crab. Lift off the carapace and discard. Scrape out any roe and discard the gills. Rinse well and halve each crab with a cleaver.
2 In a large saucepan or stockpot, bring the crabs and water to a boil over high heat. Reduce heat to medium, season with the sugar, shrimp paste and salt, and simmer for about 5 minutes. Remove the crab from the soup and set aside to cool. Keep the soup hot over very low heat.
3 Crack the crab shells and remove the crabmeat from the shells. Discard the shells.
4 Heat the oil in a wok or skillet over medium heat. Pan-fry the tofu cubes until golden brown, about 2 minutes on each side. Remove and set aside. Reheat the oil and stir-fry the garlic until golden brown and fragrant, about 1 to 2 minutes. Add the baby leek and tomato and stir-fry until tender. Season with the fish sauce and tamarind juice. Remove from the heat and add the mixture to the hot soup.
5 Bring a separate pot of water to a boil. Boil the dried rice noodles until soft, 5 to 7 minutes or longer as needed. Remove and rinse with cold water, then drain.
6 Place the rice noodles and fried tofu in individual serving bowls. Top with some crabmeat and pour the hot soup over. Garnish with spring onion and coriander leaves (cilantro), and serve hot with the Accompaniments.

Serves 4 to 6   Preparation time: 40 mins   Cooking time: 30 mins

Cabbage Roll Soup   Canh Bap Cai Cuon Thit

This classic soup is very popular during Tet, the Vietnamese New Year celebration.

1 cup (7 oz/200 g) ground pork
4 fresh medium shrimp (4 oz/100 g), peeled, deveined and mashed or ground in a food processor to yield about $1/2$ cup
4 tablespoons minced shallots (about 6 shallots)
3 tablespoons minced coriander leaves (cilantro)
$1/2$ teaspoon salt
$1/2$ teaspoon ground white pepper
1 lb (500 g) large cabbage leaves (see note), blanched until soft
10 whole spring onion greens, blanched until soft, for fastening
6 cups ($1^1/_2$ liters) chicken or pork stock or 2 to 3 stock cubes dissolved in 6 cups ($1^1/_2$ liters) hot water
2 tablespoons sliced spring onions, to garnish
Ground white pepper
2 tablespoons fish sauce, for dipping

1 Combine the pork, shrimp, shallots and $1/2$ of the coriander leaves (cilantro) in a large bowl and mix well, then season with the salt and pepper.
2 Place a heaping tablespoon of the mixture onto a blanched cabbage leaf. Fold one end of the leaf over the mixture, then fold in the sides and roll up tightly. Tie the roll securely with a spring onion green. Repeat with the remaining ingredients to make a total of 10 rolls.
3 Bring the chicken stock to a boil in a pot. Add the cabbage rolls and simmer for about 5 minutes until cooked. Remove from the heat.
4 Serve the soup in individual serving bowls with a sprinkling of spring onion and pepper, and fish sauce as the dip.

Note: The cabbage should be blanched in a pot of boiling water (not in the stock) for 3 to 4 minutes, to soften it for wrapping.

Makes 10 rolls   Preparation time: 25 mins   Cooking time: 10 mins

Preserved Pork Head Meat   Dua Dau Heo

2 teaspoons baking soda
1 cup (250 ml) water
1 lb (500 g) pig's head or collar meat
$1^1/_2$ cups (375 ml) white vinegar
2 tablespoons sugar
1 tablespoon salt
2 cloves garlic, crushed
1 finger-length red chili, deseeded and sliced
1 teaspoon black peppercorns
1 in ($2^1/_2$ cm) fresh ginger root, peeled and thinly sliced
1 tablespoon thinly sliced garlic
1 finger-length red chili, deseeded and cut into strips, to garnish

1 Mix the baking soda with the water. Briefly soak the pig's head or collar meat in the mixture, then rinse and drain. Boil the pork in a pot of lightly salted water for about 20 minutes until thoroughly cooked. Remove and set aside to cool. Cut the pig's heat meat into pieces, rinse with cold water and drain. If using collar meat, cut it into chunks.
2 In a small pot or saucepan, bring the vinegar, sugar and salt to a boil. Remove and set aside to cool.
3 Place the pork, garlic, chili, peppercorns and ginger in a clean jar. Pour in the vinegar mixture and cover the jar tightly. Set aside for a few hours.
The preserved pork is ready to be served when it is white and crunchy, and has a little sweet and sour taste.
4 To serve, slice the preserved pork into very thin slices, combine with the sliced garlic and garnish with chili.

Serves 4   Preparation time: 20 mins   Cooking time: 8 mins

Clam Soup with Starfruit and Herbs Canh Nghieu

This unusual recipe is quite easy to prepare, and like many of the soups in Vietnam, relies heavily on fresh ingredients. Starfruit, also known as carambola, is increasingly available in specialty food shops. Thin slices of fresh, tart pineapple may be used if starfruit is not available.

2 lbs (1 kg) fresh unshucked clams
4 cups (1 liter) chicken stock or 1 to 2 chicken stock cubes dissolved in 4 cups
  (1 liter) hot water
1 tablespoon oil
2 tablespoons minced baby leeks or spring onions
2 cloves garlic, minced
2 tablespoons fish sauce
1 teaspoon dried shrimp paste or *belachan*, crumbled (optional)
1 medium ripe starfruit or 2 large chunks fresh pineapple, thinly sliced
1 finger-length red chili, deseeded and cut into thin strips
Sprigs of coriander leaves (cilantro), to garnish
Polygonum leaves (*rau ram*), to garnish

1 Rinse and clean the clams thoroughly in a couple of changes of water.
2 Bring the chicken stock to a boil in a stockpot. Add the clams and simmer for 2 to 3 minutes, until they are all open. Remove from the heat and set aside to cool. Remove the clams from their shells and set aside. Discard the shells. Strain the stock and return the clear soup to the pot.
3 Heat the oil in a wok or skillet over medium heat. Stir-fry the baby leeks or spring onions and garlic until fragrant, about 1 to 2 minutes. Add the clams and season with the fish sauce and shrimp paste. Remove from the heat.
4 Bring the clear soup to a boil. Add the clam mixture and starfruit or pineapple slices, mix well and remove from the heat immediately.
5 Spoon the clam soup into individual serving bowls and top with some sliced chili. Serve hot, garnished with coriander (cilantro) and polygonum leaves.

Note: This recipe is also ideal for mussels. If available, use the small, green-lipped variety. For many of the fish soups in Vietnam, chicken or pork stock are commonly used. If you prefer, a clear vegetable or fish stock may also be used for this recipe.

Serves 4   Preparation time: 15 mins   Cooking time: 10 mins

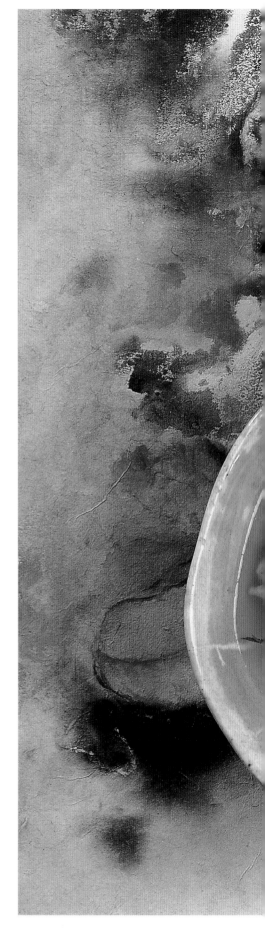

Grilled Eggplant Salad with Crabmeat

Ca Tim Nuong

This recipe is common to Cambodia and southern Vietnam and makes delicious use of eggplant, one of the many vegetables grown in central Vietnam. Shrimp or stir-fried ground pork may be used in place of the crabmeat.

1 lb (500 g) slender Asian eggplants (about 2 large or 5 small eggplants)
2 tablespoons oil
1¹/₂ cups (6 oz/175 g) cooked crabmeat
2 tablespoons Crispy Fried Shallots (page 42), to garnish
1 tablespoon thinly sliced spring onion, to garnish
Sprigs of coriander leaves (cilantro), to garnish

Dressing
1 finger-length red chili, deseeded and minced
1¹/₂ tablespoons crushed roasted unsalted peanuts
1 tablespoon fish sauce
1¹/₂ teaspoons sugar or honey
2 tablespoons water

1 Combine the Dressing ingredients in a small bowl and mix well. Set aside.
2 Halve each eggplant lengthwise and brush with a little oil. Grill, a few at a time, on a pan grill or under a preheated broiler using medium heat, turning regularly, until the skin turns brown and the flesh is tender, about 10 minutes. Remove from the heat and set aside to cool. Peel off the skin and discard.
3 Spread the crabmeat along the top of the eggplant halves and pour the Dressing over. Serve immediately, garnished with Crispy Fried Shallots (page 42), spring onion and coriander leaves (cilantro).

Serves 4 to 6   Preparation time: 25 mins   Cooking time: 10 mins

Fried Tofu with Lemongrass and Five Spice   Dau Hu Chien Sa

1 cup (250 ml) oil
4 cakes pressed tofu (about 1$^1/_2$lbs/
  600 g in total), halved and pressed
  between paper towels to remove
  moisture
2 stalks lemongrass, thick bottom
  parts only, outer layers discarded,
  inner parts minced
1 finger-length red chili, deseeded
  and minced
2 cloves garlic, minced
1 teaspoon five spice powder
$^1/_2$ teaspoon salt
$^1/_2$ teaspoon ground white pepper

1 Heat the oil in a wok or skillet over medium heat until hot. Deep-fry the tofu for about 2 minutes on each side until golden brown and crispy. Remove and drain on paper towels, then arrange on a serving platter.
2 Drain off all but 1 tablespoon of the oil in the wok or skillet. Reheat the oil over medium heat and stir-fry the minced lemongrass, chili and garlic until fragrant and tender, 1 to 2 minutes. Season with the five spice powder, salt and pepper and remove from the heat. Spread the mixture on top of the fried tofu and serve hot.

Note: Fried tofu is available in many grocery stores, which makes preparing this dish a snap. Heat the fried tofu in a microwave oven or by lightly steaming it before serving with the lemongrass-chili-garlic topping.

Makes 8 pieces   Preparation time: 10 mins   Cooking time: 10 mins

Stir-fried Vegetables with Fish Sauce   Rau Xao

12 cups (3 liters) water, with 1 teaspoon
  salt added
1 carrot, thinly sliced to yield about
  1$^1/_2$ cups
1 cup (4 oz/100 g) cauliflower florets
1 cup (3 oz/80 g) baby corn
12 fresh shiitake or dried Chinese
  black mushrooms, stems discarded
7 oz (200 g) tender kale or broccoli
  stems, sliced diagonally to yield
  about 1$^1/_2$ cups
2 tablespoons oil
1 tablespoon rice wine or sake
2 tablespoons fish sauce
2 cloves garlic, crushed
1 teaspoon ground white pepper

1 Bring the salted water to a boil in a pot and blanch the carrot, cauliflower and baby corn for about 30 seconds. Remove and plunge into cold water, then drain well.
2 Heat the oil in a wok or skillet over medium heat. Stir-fry the mushrooms and kale or broccoli stems for 1 to 2 minutes, then add the blanched vegetables, and continue to stir-fry for 2 more minutes, seasoning with the rice wine and fish sauce. Finally add the garlic, season with the pepper and remove from the heat.
3 Transfer to a serving platter and serve hot with steamed rice.

Note: When blanching, leave the vegetables in the boiling water just long enough to soften slightly, then place in the cold or ice water immediately to ensure a crisp texture. Do not overcook.

Serves 4 to 6   Preparation time: 15 mins   Cooking time: 7 mins

Pumpkin Braised in Coconut Milk   Canh Bi Ro Ham Dua

This is a traditional Buddhist vegetarian dish finished with raw peanuts and a sprinkling of fresh herbs.

13 oz (350 g) pumpkin, peeled and cubed to yield about 2 cups
8 oz (250 g) sweet potatoes or taro root, peeled and cubed to yield about 1$^1/_2$ cups
5 or 6 dried wood ear fungus, soaked in water until soft, sliced to yield about $^1/_2$ cup
$^1/_2$ cup (50 g) uncooked peanuts, soaked in warm water to soften
2 cups (500 ml) thin coconut milk
$^1/_2$ cup (80 g) sliced loofah or green zucchini
1 teaspoon sugar
$^1/_2$ teaspoon salt
2 tablespoons thinly sliced polygonum leaves (*rau ram*), to garnish
Sprigs of coriander leaves (cilantro), to garnish

1 In a pot, bring the pumpkin, sweet potato or taro root, fungus, peanuts and $^1/_2$ of the thin coconut milk to a boil over medium heat and simmer until the vegetables are tender, about 15 minutes. Add the remaining coconut milk and loofah or zucchini, and bring the mixture to a boil again. Simmer for about 10 minutes, seasoning with the sugar and salt, and remove from the heat.
2 Transfer to a serving bowl and serve hot, garnished with polygonum and coriander leaves (cilantro).

Serves 4 to 6   Preparation time: 20 mins   Cooking time: 20 mins

Stir-fried Water Spinach with Yellow Bean Sauce   Rau Muong Xao Tuong

Water spinach, which is available in many specialist Asian grocery shops, has hollow, straw-like stems that are crunchy. The best substitute is bok choy, which has a similar crunchy texture.

1 lb (500 g) water spinach (*kangkong*) or bok choy
2 tablespoons oil
2 cloves garlic, crushed
2 baby leeks or spring onions, white part thinly sliced
2 tablespoons Yellow Bean Sauce (page 26)
$^1/_4$ teaspoon salt
$^1/_4$ teaspoon ground white pepper

1 Clean the water spinach well by rinsing in water and remove the thick bottom stems. Slice or tear the upper stems and leaves into pieces.
2 Heat the oil in a wok or skillet over high heat. Stir-fry the garlic and leek for about 30 seconds until fragrant and tender. Add the spinach and Yellow Bean Sauce (page 24), and mix well. Season with the salt and pepper, then remove from the heat.
3 Transfer to a serving platter and serve hot with steamed rice.

Serves 4   Preparation time: 15 mins   Cooking time: 5 mins

Clam Rice   Com Nghieu

2 lbs (1 kg) fresh unshucked clams
$1/2$ cup (125 ml) water
1 cup (250 ml) oil
2 tablespoons pork cracklings or
  thinly sliced bacon
1 tablespoon minced garlic
2 tablespoons roasted sesame seeds
4 cups (800 g) cooked rice
2 teaspoons salt
$1/2$ teaspoon ground white pepper
4 oz (100 g) pork belly, poached for
  about 5 minutes until cooked and
  thinly sliced
1 cup (5 oz/150 g) sliced banana
  blossom (page 18) or cabbage
1 ripe starfruit (about 7 oz/200 g) or
  2 chunks pineapple, thinly sliced
2 tablespoons minced polygonum
  leaves (rau ram)
Sesame seed rice crackers, baked
  and broken into small pieces to
  yield about 1 cup

Chili Sauce
2 tablespoons bottled chili sauce
1 teaspoon dried shrimp paste or
  belachan, crumbled
1 tablespoon vinegar
1 teaspoon freshly squeezed
  lime juice
1 teaspoon sugar

1 Combine the Chili Sauce ingredients in a bowl and mix well. Transfer to a serving bowl and set aside.
2 Bring the clams and water to a boil in a covered pot or steam until they are all open, about 3 minutes. Remove from the heat and set aside to cool. Strain the stock and remove the clams from their shells. Discard the shells.
3 Heat the oil in a wok or skillet. Deep-fry the pork cracklings over low heat for about 5 minutes, stirring occasionally, until crispy and golden brown. Remove and drain on paper towels. If using the bacon, pan-fry in a skillet over low heat for 2 to 3 minutes until cooked.
4 Drain off all but 2 tablespoons of the oil in the wok or skillet. Reheat the oil over medium heat and stir-fry the minced garlic until golden brown and fragrant, 1 to 2 minutes. Add the sesame seeds and stir-fry for about 3 minutes until the sesame seeds are lightly browned. Increase the heat to high, add the rice and stir-fry for about 3 minutes until heated through, seasoning with the clam stock, salt and pepper. Add the cooked clams, mix well and remove from the heat.
5 Place the clam rice on a serving platter and arrange the pork cracklings or bacon, sliced pork, banana blossom or cabbage, sliced starfruit or pineapple, polygonum leaves and sesame seed rice cracker on top. Serve hot with a bowl of the Chili Sauce on the side.

Serves 6   Preparation time: 30 mins   Cooking time: 12 mins

Imperial Fried Rice   Com Hoang Bao

2 tablespoons oil
3 shallots, minced
4 oz (100 g) pork or chicken, diced
  to yield about 1 cup
4 fresh medium shrimp (4 oz/100 g),
  peeled and deveined
$3/4$ cup (4 oz/100 g) dried lotus
  seeds, boiled for 20 minutes to soft-
  en and drained
1 teaspoon salt
1 teaspoon ground white pepper
2 cups (400 g) cooked rice
1 egg, fried and diced (optional)
1 baby leek or spring onion, sliced

1 Heat the oil in a wok or skillet over medium heat. Stir-fry the shallots for 1 to 2 minutes until fragrant and translucent. Increase the heat to high, add the pork or chicken, shrimp, lotus seeds, salt and pepper, and stir-fry to mix well, 1 to 2 minutes. Add the rice and egg (if using), and continue to stir-fry until heated through and well blended, about 2 minutes. Remove from the heat and place on a serving platter
2 Sprinkle the baby leek or spring onion on top of the fried rice and serve hot.

Note: Traditionally in Vietnam, Imperial Fried Rice is served wrapped in a lotus leaf, as shown in the photo. The leaf imparts a wonderful fresh fragrance to the rice. Place the fried rice on a large piece of lotus leaf while it is still hot. Wrap by folding the lotus leaf into a neat package. Set the package aside for about 10 minutes before serving.

Serves 4   Preparation time: 20 mins   Cooking time: 30 mins

Vietnamese Fish Stew Mam Kho

This is a hearty soup recipe that calls for dried salted fish, considered a delicacy in Vietnam.

2 tablespoons oil
3 cloves garlic, minced
$^1/_2$ cup (4 oz/100 g) minced shallots
  (about 12 shallots)
2 oz (50 g) pork belly, sliced
1 slender Asian eggplant (5 oz/150 g),
  cubed
3 stalks lemongrass, thick bottom parts
  only, outer layers discarded, inner
  parts minced
$^1/_2$ teaspoon crushed black peppercorns
3 cups (750 ml) water
7 oz (200 g) dried salted fish (see note)
10 oz (300 g) fresh fish fillets (halibut,
  mackerel, swordfish or catfish)
2 finger-length red chilies, deseeded
  and sliced
2 teaspoons sugar
4 fresh medium shrimp (about 4 oz/
  100 g), peeled and deveined
1 tablespoon thinly sliced spring onion
1 tablespoon Crispy Fried Shallots
  (page 42), to garnish

1 Heat the oil in a wok or skillet over medium heat. Stir-fry the garlic, shallots, pork, eggplant, lemongrass and peppercorns for about 5 minutes, until cooked. Remove from the heat and set aside.
2 In a large saucepan, bring the water, salted fish and fresh fish to a boil over medium heat, then simmer for about 10 minutes and remove from the heat. Remove the fish and set aside. Strain the stock.
3 Bring the clear stock to a boil again in a pot. Add the stir-fried pork mixture, chilies and sugar, and simmer over medium heat for about 5 minutes or until the soup has reduced by one-third. Finally, add the shrimp and simmer for 3 more minutes until they turn pink, then remove from the heat.
4 Place the fish in individual serving bowls. Pour the stew over and sprinkle with spring onion and Crispy Fried Shallots (page 26).

Note: There are many different grades of dried salted fish and the better ones can be quite expensive, however, any dried or salted fish will work with this recipe—salt cod is a good choice. Rinse and clean the salted fish thoroughly. Soak for 10 to 15 minutes. Soak for a longer period of time or overnight for a more subtle flavor, or to remove more of the salt.

Serves 4   Preparation time: 30 mins   Cooking time: 25 mins

Sweet and Sour Fish Soup   Canh Chua Ca Loc

Also known as Vietnamese tamarind fish soup, this dish is a light and refreshingly fragrant soup, making use of fresh herbs and pineapple. The recipe calls for the firm white-fleshed mullet, also called mud-fish, which has a strong "fishy" flavor. Red snapper or catfish fillets may also be used.

4 cups (1 liter) water
1 lb (500 g) fresh snapper, mullet or catfish fillets, cut into pieces
1/2 cup (75 g) sliced pineapple
1 finger-length red chili, deseeded and sliced
2 okra (lady's fingers), sliced
1/2 cup (75 g) sliced taro stems or celery
1/2 cup (125 ml) tamarind juice (page 22)
1/4 cup (10 g) bean sprouts
1 ripe tomato, cut into wedges
3 tablespoons fish sauce
1 tablespoon sugar
1 tablespoon Crispy Fried Shallots (page 42)
2 tablespoons minced mint leaves (about 40 leaves/5 g)
Sprigs of coriander leaves (cilantro), to garnish

1 Bring the water to a boil in a saucepan and poach the fish for 3 to 5 minutes until just cooked. Remove from the heat and transfer the fish to a large serving bowl. Strain the fish stock.
2 Return the clear fish stock to the pan and bring to a boil again over high heat. Add the pineapple, chili, okra and taro stems or celery, and mix well. Reduce the heat to medium and simmer for 3 to 4 minutes. Add the tamarind juice, bean sprouts and tomato, and bring the mixture to a boil again, skimming off any foam that floats to the surface. Season the soup with the fish sauce and sugar, and remove from the heat.
3 Pour the hot soup over the fish and top with Crispy Fried Shallots (page 42), mint leaves and coriander leaves (cilantro). Serve hot.

Note: If using canned pineapple, drain the syrup and reduce the amount of sugar used.

Serves 4   Preparation time: 30 mins   Cooking time: 10 mins

Stuffed Squid   Muc Nhoi Thit

8 fresh medium squids or 4 large
   squids (about 2 lbs/1 kg)
Toothpicks, for fastening
4 tablespoons butter or oil
2 tablespoons diced shallots (about
   3 shallots)
3 cloves garlic, crushed

Filling
1 tablespoon oil
2 tablespoons thinly sliced shallots
   (about 3 shallots)
1 clove garlic, thinly sliced
10 oz (300 g) lean ground pork
1 oz (25 g) dried glass noodles,
   soaked in water until soft, drained
   and cut into thirds to yield $1/4$ cup
6 wood ear fungus, soaked in water
   until soft, sliced
$1/4$ teaspoon five spice powder
1 tablespoon soy sauce
$3/4$ teaspoon salt
$1/2$ teaspoon ground white pepper
1 teaspoon sugar

Tomato Lime Sauce
3 large ripe tomatoes, blanched,
   skinned and deseeded, flesh diced
   (or use 1 cup canned stewed tomatoes)
4 tablespoons minced coriander
   leaves (cilantro)
4 tablespoons minced parsley
$1/2$ tablespoon fish sauce
1 teaspoon sugar
1 tablespoon freshly squeezed
   lime juice
$1/4$ teaspoon ground white pepper

1 Rinse each squid thoroughly, detaching and discarding the head. Remove the cartilage in the center of the tentacles and mince the tentacles. Remove the reddish-brown skin from the body sac and scrape the inside of the body sac with the dull edge of a knife. Rinse well.

2 To make the Filling, heat the oil in a wok or skillet over medium heat and stir-fry the shallots and garlic until golden brown and fragrant, 1 to 2 minutes. Remove from the heat and transfer to a bowl. Combine with the minced tentacles and all the other ingredients and mix well.

3 Stuff each body sac with the Filling and secure with a toothpick. Place all the stuffed squid on a plate and set aside.

4 Heat the butter or oil in a wok or skillet over medium heat and stir-fry the shallots and garlic until fragrant, 1 to 2 minutes. Add the stuffed squid, a few at a time, and pan-fry for about 5 minutes on each side, until slightly brown and cooked through. Remove the stuffed squid from the heat and set aside to cool. Add the Tomato Lime Sauce ingredients to the wok or skillet and simmer until the tomato is tender and the sauce is thick, then remove from the heat.

5 Remove the toothpicks and slice the stuffed squids into disks. Place on a serving platter, spread the Tomato Lime Sauce over and serve hot.

Note: For an interesting variation, try grilling the stuffed squid.

Serves 6   Preparation time: 45 mins   Cooking time: 15 mins

Marinated Grilled Squid   Muc Nuong

Grilled meats and seafood are very popular in Vietnam. This recipe uses a flexible Marinade, which also works well with many other types of seafood or poultry prior to grilling.

1 lb (500 g) fresh medium squids, body sacs only
$1/_2$ tablespoon salt
Sprigs of coriander leaves (cilantro), to garnish
Fish Sauce Dip (page 26), for dipping

Marinade
$1/_2$ teaspoon ground white pepper
2 cloves garlic, crushed
2 tablespoons oil
1 teaspoon five spice powder
1 teaspoon curry powder
1 tablespoon minced lemongrass (from inner part of the thick end of the stalk)
1 tablespoon black soy sauce
1 teaspoon sesame oil
1 tablespoon freshly squeezed lime juice
1 teaspoon sugar

1 Make a lengthwise cut along each squid body sac. Open up and rinse the inside well. Score the flesh by making diagonal criss-cross slits across the surface. This allows the squid to cook very quickly. Slice into bite-sized pieces.
2 Rub the salt onto the squid pieces. Set aside for about 15 minutes, then rinse and drain.
3 Combine the Marinade ingredients in a bowl and mix well. Place the squid pieces in the Marinade, mix until well coated and marinate for at least 1 hour.
4 Grill the marinated squid pieces on a pan grill or under a preheated broiler using high heat until just cooked, about 2 minutes on each side.
5 Arrange the grilled squid on a serving platter and garnish with coriander leaves (cilantro). Serve hot with a bowl of Fish Sauce Dip (page 26) on the side.

Serves 4   Preparation time: 30 mins   Cooking time: 5 mins

Spicy Jumbo Shrimp   Tom Cang Kho

This is a southern Vietnamese recipe that calls for jumbo shrimp, which are often almost as big as lobsters. Smaller shrimp, crayfish or baby lobsters can also be used.

1 tablespoon oil
3 cloves garlic, minced
1 finger-length red chili, deseeded and minced
1 teaspoon crushed black peppercorns
1$\frac{1}{2}$ tablespoons sugar
3 tablespoons fish sauce
$\frac{1}{2}$ cup (125 ml) water
6 fresh giant shrimp (about 1$\frac{1}{2}$ lbs/ 600 g in total)
4 tablespoons minced coriander leaves (cilantro), to garnish

1 Heat the oil in a wok or skillet over medium heat. Stir-fry the garlic and chili until fragrant and soft, 1 to 2 minutes. Add the black peppercorns, sugar, fish sauce and water, and mix well. Add the shrimp and simmer uncovered for 7 to 10 minutes, basting frequently with the sauce, until the shrimp turn pink and are just cooked. Remove the shrimp and arrange them on a serving platter.

2 Reduce the heat to low and continue to simmer the sauce until it thickens, 3 to 5 minutes. Remove from the heat and pour the sauce over the shrimp and garnish with coriander leaves (cilantro). Serve hot.

Serves 6   Preparation time: 10 mins   Cooking time: 10 mins

Stir-fried Squid with Vegetables and Pineapple   Muc Xao Thap Cam

3 tablespoons oil
3 cloves garlic, minced
1 lb (500 g) fresh medium squids, cleaned and cut into bite-sized pieces
1 medium carrot, sliced
$\frac{1}{2}$ stalk celery (80 g), diced to yield about $\frac{1}{2}$ cup
1 medium onion, cut into wedges
1 cup (4 oz/100 g) snow peas
$\frac{3}{4}$ teaspoon salt
2 teaspoons crushed black peppercorns
2 ripe medium tomatoes, cut into wedges
1$\frac{1}{2}$ cups (10 oz/300 g) pineapple chunks
2 tablespoons fish sauce
$\frac{1}{4}$ teaspoon ground white pepper
1 tablespoon minced coriander leaves (cilantro), to garnish

1 Heat 2 tablespoons of the oil in a wok or skillet over medium heat. Stir-fry $\frac{1}{2}$ of the garlic until golden brown and fragrant, 1 to 2 minutes. Add the squid pieces and stir-fry for 1 to 2 minutes, until just cooked. Remove from the pan and set aside.

2 Heat the remaining oil in the wok or skillet over medium heat and stir-fry the remaining garlic until golden brown and fragrant, 1 to 2 minutes. Add the carrot, celery, onion and snow peas, and stir-fry for 2 to 3 minutes, seasoning with the salt and pepper, until the vegetables are tender. Finally add the tomatoes, pineapple, cooked squid and fish sauce, and continue stir-frying for another minute before removing from the heat.

3 Transfer to a serving platter, sprinkle with pepper and garnish with coriander leaves (cilantro). Serve hot with steamed rice.

Serves 6   Preparation time: 30 mins   Cooking time: 10 mins

Crabs with Tamarind Sauce   Cua Rang Vot Sot Me

This is what they're eating at those crowded tables on the sidewalks of Ho Chi Minh City—a taste sensation!

3 lbs (1¹/₄ kg) fresh medium crabs
  (about 3 to 4 crabs)
Oil for deep-frying
1 tablespoon tamarind pulp
¹/₂ cup (125 ml) rice wine or sherry
4 cloves garlic, minced
2 tablespoons fish sauce
1 teaspoon ground white pepper
2 baby leeks or spring onions, cut
  into lengths
¹/₄ cup (60 ml) water

1 Scrub and rinse the crabs thoroughly. Detach the claws from each crab. Lift off the carapace and discard. Scrape out any roe and discard the gills. Rinse well, halve the crabs with a cleaver and crack the claws with a mallet. Pat dry with paper towels.
2 Heat the oil in a wok until very hot. Deep-fry the crabs for about 30 seconds, until the color changes. Remove and drain on paper towels.
3 Mix the tamarind pulp with rice wine in a bowl. Mash well and strain through a sieve. Discard the seeds and fibers. Set aside.
4 Heat 2 tablespoons of the oil in a wok over medium heat. Stir-fry the garlic for 1 to 2 minutes until fragrant and golden brown. Increase the heat to high, add the deep-fried crabs and stir-fry for 2 to 3 minutes, seasoning with the tamarind mixture, fish sauce and pepper. Reduce the heat to low and stir-fry for 2 more minutes. Finally add the leeks or spring onions and water, mix well and remove from the heat. Serve immediately with steamed rice.

Note: A large wire strainer with a handle is very useful for lifting the crabs out of the wok. Or if you have a deep-fryer, this makes the cooking easier. You can substitute freshly ground black pepper for white pepper although the latter is often the preferred ingredient of Vietnamese cooks.

Serves 4 to 6   Preparation time: 20 mins   Cooking time: 10 mins

Crabs Simmered in Beer   Cua Hap Bia

Beer is a popular drink in Vietnam, but it also makes for a delicious broth. This is an innovative dish said to have been developed by an early French colonial administrator.

3 lbs (1¹/₄ kg) fresh medium crabs
  (about 3 to 4 crabs)
2 tablespoons oil
1 clove garlic, crushed
1 teaspoon sesame oil
1 tablespoon oyster sauce
¹/₂ teaspoon salt
¹/₂ teaspoon ground white pepper
1 large onion, cut into wedges
1 ripe tomato, cut into wedges
1 finger-length red chili, deseeded
  and sliced
³/₄ cup (185 ml) beer
Crispy Fried Shallots (page 42)
  (optional)
Sprigs of watercress, to garnish

1 Scrub and rinse the crabs thoroughly. Detach the claws from each crab. Lift off the carapace and discard. Scrape out any roe and discard the gills. Rinse well, halve the crabs with a cleaver and crack the claws with a mallet.
2 Heat the oil in a wok over medium heat and stir-fry the garlic until golden brown and fragrant, 1 to 2 minutes. Increase the heat to high, add the crabs and stir-fry for about 5 minutes, seasoning with the sesame oil, oyster sauce, salt and pepper. Add the onion, tomato and chili, and mix well. Reduce the heat to medium, add the beer, cover the wok and simmer for about 10 minutes until the crabs are cooked. Remove from the heat.
3 Transfer to a serving platter, sprinkle with Crispy Fried Shallots (if using) and garnish with watercress. Serve hot.

Note: Almost any variety of hard shell crab can be used for this recipe.

Serves 4 to 6   Preparation time: 20 mins   Cooking time: 20 mins

Crisp Soft-shell Crabs, Oysters and Clams with Sweet and Sour Sauce

Cua Va Nghieu Lan Bot Chien Gion

This is a dish that can be served as a main course or an appetizer. It's similar to English fish and chips but with an Asian twist.

12 large fresh unshucked clams
12 freshly shucked oysters
6 soft-shell crabs, cleaned and trimmed
Oil for deep-frying
3 tablespoons flour, for dusting
3 large cabbage leaves, to serve
Sweet and Sour Sauce (page 27), for dipping

Marinade
1 teaspoon sesame oil
2 cloves garlic, crushed
2 teaspoons ground white pepper
1 teaspoon salt

Batter
1 cup (150 g) flour
1 cup (125 g) rice flour
1 cup (250 ml) water
1 tablespoon vinegar
2 tablespoons soy sauce
1 teaspoon annatto seed oil (page 51)
1 teaspoon sugar

1 Soak and wash the clams in a couple of changes of water. Boil in a pot of water for 3 to 5 minutes until they are all open. Remove and set aside to cool. Remove the clams from their shells and discard the shells.
2 Combine the Marinade ingredients in a large bowl and mix well. Add the clams, oysters and crabs, and mix until well-coated. Allow to marinate for at least 45 minutes.
3 Make the Batter by combining all the ingredients in a bowl and mixing thoroughly until a smooth thick batter (with a consistency of pancake batter) is obtained, adding more flour or water as needed.
4 Heat the oil in a wok or pot over medium heat until hot. Working with a few pieces at a time, lightly dust the marinated seafood with a little flour, then dip them into the Batter, ensuring they are evenly coated. Gently lower the coated seafood pieces into the hot oil and deep-fry for about 3 minutes on each side, until crispy and golden brown. Remove and drain on paper towels.
5 Line a serving platter with cabbage leaves and arrange the deep-fried seafood on top. Serve with a bowl of Sweet and Sour Sauce (page 27) on the side.

Note: Soft-shell crabs are freshly molted crabs with their new shell still tender and flexible. The blue crab is most commonly eaten in its soft-shell state. Normally sold fresh, buy crabs that are firm and do not smell unpleasant. If unavailable, you may use shrimp in place of the crabs.

Serves 8   Preparation time: 30 mins + 45 mins to marinate   Cooking time: 20 mins

Whole Fish with Ginger Lemongrass Sauce   Ca Mu Chien Voi Gung

Vietnam boasts an abundance of ocean and fresh-water fish. Ginger and galangal, both members of the ginger family, are used to impart their unique flavors to these fish dishes.

1 fresh grouper, snapper or sea bass
   (about 1$^1/_2$ lbs/750 g)
$^1/_4$ teaspoon salt
$^1/_2$ teaspoon ground white pepper
1 tablespoon oil
1 tablespoon sliced spring onion, to
   garnish

Sauce
1 tablespoon oil
3 fresh shiitake mushrooms, stems
   discarded, caps thinly sliced
1$^1/_2$ in (4 cm) fresh ginger root,
   peeled and cut into thin shreds
1 tablespoon minced lemongrass
   (from inner part of the thick end of
   the stalk)
1 finger-length red chili, deseeded
   and cut into thin strips
1 teaspoon soy sauce
2 tablespoons fish sauce
$^1/_2$ cup (125 ml) water

1 Clean and pat the fish dry with paper towels. Rub the salt and pepper onto the fish and brush with a little oil. Grill the fish on a pan grill or under a preheated broiler using medium heat for about 7 minutes on each side, until the fish is cooked. Alternatively, you can shallow-fry the fish in a wok or skillet using 4 tablespoons of oil for 3 to 5 minutes on each side until crispy and cooked. Remove and transfer the fish to a serving platter.
2 Combine the Sauce ingredients in a saucepan and simmer over low heat for about 5 minutes. Remove and pour the Sauce over the fish.
3 Garnish the fish with spring onion and serve hot.

Note: Canned straw mushrooms or dried black Chinese mushrooms can be substituted for fresh shiitake. Soak dried black Chinese mushrooms in water to soften before using.

Serves 4   Preparation time: 20 mins   Cooking time: 15 mins

Braised Fish with Galangal Sauce   Ca Chep Kho Rieng

3 tablespoons oil
6 fish steaks (halibut, swordfish or
   carp, each about 4 oz/100 g)
1$^1/_2$ in (4 cm) fresh galangal root,
   peeled and cut into thin strips
2 tablespoons fish sauce
1 tablespoon Caramel Syrup
   (page 27)
$^1/_2$ cup (125 ml) water

1 Heat the oil in a wok or skillet over medium heat. Stir-fry the galangal until golden brown and fragrant, about 1 to 2 minutes. Add the fish steaks and pan-fry for 2 to 3 minutes on each side. Add the fish sauce, Caramel Syrup (page 27) and water, and braise the fish uncovered until cooked, about 5 minutes. Remove from the heat.
2 Arrange on a serving platter and serve hot with steamed rice.

Serves 4 to 6   Preparation time: 10 mins   Cooking time: 10 mins

Minced Salmon with Sesame Seed Rice Crackers
Luon Xao Lan Xuc Banh Trang Me

This recipe was created as an appetizer or a party snack to go with those delightful sesame seed rice crackers—the mixture is perfect for dipping into.

2 tablespoons oil
1 tablespoon minced garlic
2 tablespoons diced shallots (about 3 shallots)
2 tablespoons minced lemongrass (from inner part of the thick end of the stalk)
1 tablespoon minced red chili
5 to 6 dried wood ear fungus, soaked in water until soft, finely minced
1 tablespoon five spice powder
1 tablespoon curry powder
10 oz (300 g) diced salmon fillets or ground chicken
2 tablespoons crushed roasted unsalted peanuts
Sprigs of coriander leaves (cilantro), to garnish
1 finger-length red chili, deseeded and cut into thin strips, to garnish
Sesame seed rice crackers, to serve

1 Heat the oil in a wok or skillet over medium heat. Stir-fry the garlic, shallots, lemongrass, chili and fungus for 1 to 2 minutes until fragrant. Add the five spice powder and curry powder, followed by the salmon or chicken, and stir-fry for about 5 minutes, until cooked. Remove from the heat.
2 Transfer to a serving platter and top with peanuts. Garnish with coriander leaves (cilantro) and chili, and serve with sesame seed rice crackers.

Note: Wood ear fungus are used for their texture. However, any fresh mushroom that adds texture and flavor is a good substitute. Some dried varieties will also work.

Serves 4   Preparation time: 25 mins   Cooking time: 10 mins

River Fish Stew with Dill and Tomato   Ca Nau Ngot

6 cups (1¹/₂ liters) chicken stock or 2 to 3 chicken stock cubes dissolved in 6 cups (1¹/₂ liters) hot water
1 lb (500 g) freshwater fish fillets, cut into chunks
2 ripe medium tomatoes, cut into wedges
1 tablespoon minced dill
1 teaspoon salt
¹/₂ teaspoon ground white pepper
Fresh dill, to garnish

1 Bring the chicken stock to a boil in a pot. Add the fish and simmer for about 5 minutes, skimming off any foam that floats to the surface, then add the tomato and chopped dill, seasoning with the salt and pepper. Simmer for another 2 to 3 minutes and remove from the heat.
2 Serve hot in individual serving bowls, garnished with fresh dill.

Serves 4   Preparation time: 5 mins   Cooking time: 10 mins

Braised Duck with Ginger Vit Kho Gung

4 in (10 cm) fresh ginger root, peeled
  and cut into thin strips
$3/_4$ tablespoon salt
1 fresh duck (about $4^1/_2$ lbs/2 kg)
2 tablespoons oil
2 tablespoons fish sauce
1 tablespoon sugar
2 cups (500 ml) boiling water
1 finger-length red chili, deseeded
  and sliced
1 teaspoon ground white pepper
Sprigs of celery leaves, to garnish

1. Rub $1/_2$ of the ginger and the salt onto the duck. Set aside for 15 minutes, then rinse and drain. Cut the duck into 8 pieces.
2. Heat the oil in a wok or large skillet over medium heat until hot. Pan-fry the duck pieces for about 7 minutes on each side, until browned. Remove from the heat and drain on paper towels.
3. Drain off all but 1 tablespoon of the oil in the wok. Reheat the oil over medium heat and stir-fry the remaining ginger for 1 to 2 minutes, until fragrant. Add the fried duck pieces and season with the fish sauce and sugar, then pour in the boiling water. Add the chili and pepper, mix well and simmer covered for about 30 minutes. Reduce the heat to low, simmer uncovered for another 30 minutes, stirring occasionally, until the duck pieces are tender, then remove from the heat.
4 Transfer to a serving bowl and serve hot, garnished with celery leaves.

Serves 6 to 8   Preparation time: 30 mins   Cooking time: 1 hour 15 mins

Banana Blossom Salad with Duck Goi Vit Bap Chuoi

1 young banana blossom (page 18),
  sliced to yield $1^1/_2$ cups
2 cups (500 ml) ice water
1 tablespoon freshly squeezed
  lemon juice
2 duck breasts
$1/_4$ cup (60 ml) Fish Sauce Dip
  (page 26)
1 teaspoon thinly sliced polygonum
  leaves (rau ram)
1 in ($2^1/_2$ cm) fresh ginger root,
  peeled and minced
1 tablespoon crushed roasted unsalted peanuts
1 tablespoon Crispy Fried Shallots
  (page 42), to garnish

1 Boil the sliced banana blossom in a pot of water until tender, about 20 minutes. Remove and soak in the ice water with lemon juice for about 1 hour, then squeeze until dry and set aside.
2 Place the duck in a saucepan and cover with $3/_4$ cup of water. Poach over medium low heat for about 30 minutes. Remove from the heat and set aside to cool, then shred the duck along the grain into thin strips.
3 Combine the banana blossom, duck, Fish Sauce Dip (page 26), polygonum leaves, ginger and peanuts in a large bowl, and toss until well blended.
4 Arrange the salad on a serving platter and sprinkle with the Crispy Fried Shallots (page 42) on top. Serve immediately.

Note: If banana blossom is not available, use $1^1/_2$ cups shaved celery instead. Do not boil the celery but toss the fresh celery with all the other ingredients. Alternatively, the duck breasts can be steamed, baked, fried or grilled.

Serves 4   Preparation time: 45 mins + 1 hour soaking   Cooking time: 50 mins

Honey Roasted Chicken   Ga Quay Mat Ong

This recipe works well with any type of fowl or game. Since considerable time is involved in the glazing and cooking, it is probably best suited to a large bird and a special occasion.

2 tablespoons sugar
2 teaspoons sesame oil
2 teaspoons salt
2 teaspoons ground white pepper
1 fresh chicken (about 3 lbs/1$^1\!/_4$ kg)
Cucumber and tomato slices,
  to garnish

Honey Glaze
3 tablespoons honey
2 tablespoons sweet black soy sauce
1 tablespoon freshly squeezed
  lime juice
1 tablespoon annatto seed oil
  (page 51) (optional)
1 teaspoon sesame oil

1 Combine the sugar, sesame oil, salt and pepper in a bowl, and mix well. Rub the mixture onto the outside and inside of the chicken. Seal the cavity with a skewer and set aside for at least 1 hour.
2 Preheat the oven to 375°F (190°C).
3 Combine the Honey Glaze ingredients in a bowl and mix well.
4 Place the chicken on a roasting pan and spread $^1\!/_2$ of the Honey Glaze over the chicken. Roast the chicken in the oven for about 40 minutes, basting with the remaining Honey Glaze every 10 to 15 minutes, until golden brown and well cooked.
5 Cut the chicken into pieces and serve hot with cucumber and tomato slices.

Serves 4 to 6   Preparation time: 5 mins   Cooking time: 40 mins

Chicken Curry in Coconut Milk Ca Ri Ga Nuoc Cot Dua

Curried dishes have traditionally been associated with Thais and Cambodians or Cham minorities in Vietnam, and there are a number of popular recipes where curry powder is the featured spice. This is one of the best.

1¹/₂ lbs (750 g) chicken breasts or thighs, cut into bite-sized pieces
1 tablespoon oil
3 cloves garlic, minced
1 tablespoon curry powder
1 medium onion, cut into wedges
1 finger-length red chili, deseeded and sliced
1 stalk lemongrass, inner part bruised
1 tablespoon sugar
1 teaspoon salt
¹/₂ tablespoon ground white pepper
³/₄ cup (185 ml) thin coconut milk
7 oz (200 g) sweet potatoes or potatoes, peeled and cubed

Marinade
2 cloves garlic, crushed
1 tablespoon minced lemongrass
1 in (2¹/₂ cm) fresh ginger root, peeled and minced
2 tablespoons curry powder

1 Combine the Marinade ingredients in a mixing bowl and mix well. Add the chicken pieces, mix until well coated and allow to marinate for at least 1 hour.
2 Heat the oil in a wok or skillet over high heat, stir-fry the garlic, curry powder, onion, chili and lemongrass for about 2 minutes, until fragrant. Add the marinated chicken and stir-fry for about 5 minutes, seasoning with the sugar, salt and pepper. Add the coconut milk, reduce the heat to medium and bring slowly to a boil, then add the sweet potatoes or potatoes and simmer for about 10 minutes, until tender. Remove from the heat.
3 Discard the lemongrass, transfer to individual serving bowls and serve immediately.

Note: French bread or a baguette is delicious with this curry, along with chilies and Salt, Pepper and Lime Mix (page 27).

Serves 4 to 6   Preparation time: 30 mins   Cooking time: 15 mins

Spicy Duck in Orange Sauce   Vit Nau Cam

1 fresh duck (about 4¹/₂ lbs/2 kg),
  cut into pieces
1 cup (250 ml) oil, for frying
2 finger-length red chilies, deseeded
  and sliced
2 tablespoons sugar
3 cups (750 ml) orange juice
1 fresh orange, peeled and segmented
Grated orange peel, to garnish

Marinade
1 in (2$^1/_2$ cm) fresh ginger root,
  peeled and minced
2 finger-length red chilies, deseeded
  and minced
1 tablespoon fish sauce
$^1/_2$ teaspoon salt
$^1/_2$ teaspoon ground white pepper

1 Combine the Marinade ingredients in a large bowl and mix well. Add the duck pieces, mix until well coated, and set aside to marinate for at least 1 hour.
2 Heat the oil in a wok over medium heat until hot. Reserving the Marinade, pan-fry the marinated duck pieces, a few at a time, for about 5 minutes on each side, until golden brown and cooked. Remove and drain on paper towels.
3 Drain off all but 1 tablespoon of the oil in the wok. Reheat the oil over medium heat and stir in the reserved Marinade. Add the chili and sugar, and stir-fry until the sugar begins to caramelize, then add the orange juice and fried duck pieces. Reduce the heat to low, braise the duck uncovered for about 2 hours, stirring occasionally, until the sauce has reduced and thickened. Add the orange segments before removing from the heat.
4 Transfer to a serving platter, sprinkle grated orange peel on top and serve hot with steamed rice.

Note: You may prefer to roast the duck in the oven and basting with the Marinade regularly.

Serves 8   Preparation time: 30 mins + 1 hour to marinate   Cooking time: 2$^1/_2$ hours

Stir-fried Chicken Chunks with Mango and Cashews   Ga Xao Hot Dieu

Quick deep-frying of the chicken at the beginning of this recipe produces exquisitely tender pieces of chicken, however, the chicken chunks may also be stir-fried if you prefer.

Oil for deep-frying
4 chicken breasts (about 1lb/500 g),
  cut into chunks
1 tablespoon minced garlic
1 finger-length red chili, deseeded
  and sliced
$^3/_4$ cup (80 g) snow peas
1 tablespoon fish sauce
1 teaspoon freshly squeezed lime juice
1 teaspoon sugar
$^1/_4$ teaspoon ground white pepper
1 small ripe mango, peeled, pitted
  and sliced to yield about $^3/_4$ cup
1 ripe tomato, blanched and peeled,
  then deseeded and diced to yield
  about $^1/_3$ cup, or alternatively,
  use $^1/_3$ cup stewed or peeled
  canned tomatoes
$^1/_3$ cup (30 g) roasted cashew nuts

1 Heat the oil in a wok over medium heat until hot. Deep-fry the chicken for 4 to 5 minutes until just cooked. Remove and drain on paper towels.
2 Drain off all but 2 tablespoons of the oil in the wok. Reheat the oil over medium heat and stir-fry the garlic and chili for 1 to 2 minutes, until fragrant and tender. Add the deep-fried chicken and snow peas, and stir-fry to mix well. Season with the fish sauce, lime juice, sugar and pepper, and remove from the heat.
3 Just before serving, add the mango, tomato and cashew nuts, mix well and transfer to a serving platter. Serve hot.

Serves 6   Preparation time: 25 mins   Cooking time: 20 mins

Sautéed Frogs' Legs or Chicken Wings with Lemongrass

Dui Ech Xao Sa Ot

Oil for deep-frying
8 pairs frogs' legs (about 12 oz/350 g), washed and halved, dried with paper towels or 8 chicken wings (about 1 lb/500 g), cut at the joints
1 stalk lemongrass, thick bottom part only, outer layers discarded, inner part minced
1 clove garlic, minced
1 finger-length red chili, deseeded and minced
1 teaspoon meat curry powder
1 tablespoon fish sauce
$1/_2$ teaspoon sugar
$1/_4$ teaspoon ground white pepper
$1/_4$ cup (60 ml) chicken stock or $1/_4$ chicken stock cube dissolved in $1/_4$ cup (60 ml) hot water
1 finger-length red chili, deseeded and cut into strips, to garnish

1 Heat the oil in a wok over medium heat until very hot. Deep-fry the frogs' legs or chicken wings for about 5 minutes until crispy. Remove and drain on paper towels.
2 Drain off all but $1^1/_2$ tablespoons of the oil in the wok. Reheat the oil over medium heat, add the lemongrass, garlic, chili and deep-fried frogs' leg or chicken wings, and stir-fry for about 30 seconds. Add the curry powder, fish sauce, sugar and pepper, followed by the chicken stock, mix well and bring to a boil. Simmer uncovered for 2 to 3 minutes and remove from the heat.
3 Transfer to a serving bowl, garnish with chili and serve hot with steamed rice.

Note: This recipe makes a great appetizer when served hot and crispy.

Serves 4 to 6   Preparation time: 10 mins   Cooking time: 15 mins

Snails Stuffed with Minced Pork   Oc Nhoi Thit

3 stalks lemongrass, thick bottom parts only, outer layers discarded, inner parts cut into lengths
Fish Sauce Dip (page 26), for dipping

Filling
18 fresh snails in shells or 1 can canned snails
5 oz (150 g) ground pork (about $3/_4$ cup)
2 to 3 dried wood ear fungus, soaked in water until soft, drained and minced
2 oz (50 g) dried glass noodles, soaked in water until soft, drained and minced
2 shallots, diced
1 stalk lemongrass, thick bottom part only, outer layers discarded, inner part minced
$1/_2$ teaspoon salt
$1/_4$ teaspoon ground white pepper
1 egg yolk

1 Make the Filling first by soaking and rinsing the fresh snails in a couple of changes of water. Boil or steam them for 5 minutes, then remove from the heat. When cool enough to handle, discard the hard end from each snail and remove the snail from its shell with a hook or a pair of tweezers. Discard the body and intestine, reserving only the foot for cooking. Mince the fresh or canned snails' feet, combine with all the other ingredients and mix well.
2 Stuff each snail shell with the Filling and insert one or two pieces of the lemongrass into the Filling. Steam the stuffed snails for about 5 minutes until cooked. If using the canned snails, place the Filling in a steaming dish and steam in the same manner.
3 Serve hot with a bowl of Fish Sauce Dip (page 26) on the side.

Note: Canned snails are generally a good product and available in many supermarkets.

Serves 4 to 6   Preparation time: 30 mins   Cooking time: 10 mins

Braised Pork with Fish Sauce   Thit Heo Kho Tieu

Here are two different and delicious recipes featuring pork and *nuoc mam*. The combination is one of the characteristic flavors of Vietnamese cuisine.

1 lb (500 g) boneless pork leg, sliced
1 cup (250 ml) water
Ground white pepper

Marinade
4 tablespoons fish sauce
1 tablespoon Caramel Syrup (page 27)
1 tablespoon crushed black peppercorns
1 finger-length red chili, deseeded and halved lengthwise
1 tablespoon sugar

1 Make the Marinade first by combining all the ingredients in a bowl and mixing well. Place the pork slices in the Marinade, mix until well coated and allow to marinate for at least 1 hour.
2 Bring the marinated pork slices and a little of the Marinade to a boil in a wok or skillet. Reduce the heat to low and simmer uncovered until the sauce almost dries up, 3 to 5 minutes. Add the water, increase the heat to medium and continue to simmer for 3 more minutes, until the pork is cooked. Remove and transfer to a serving bowl.
3 Sprinkle the braised pork with pepper and serve hot with fresh vegetables and steamed rice.

Note: Coconut juice can be used instead of water.

Serves 4   Preparation time: 15 mins + 1 hour to marinate   Cooking time: 10 mins

Pork Stewed in Coconut Juice   Thit Heo Kho Nuoc Dua

2 lbs (1 kg) boneless pork leg, cut into chunks
1 tablespoon oil
2 cups (500 ml) young coconut juice (from 1 young coconut)
5 eggs, hard-boiled and shelled (optional)

Marinade
4 cloves garlic, minced
1 tablespoon shaved palm sugar
6 tablespoons fish sauce

1 Make the Marinade by combining all the ingredients in a bowl. Place the pork in the Marinade, mix until well coated and allow to marinate for at least 1 hour.
2 Heat the oil in a wok or skillet over medium high heat until hot. Sear the marinated pork for 2 minutes on each side, until lightly browned. Add the coconut juice and bring to a boil. Reduce the heat to low and simmer uncovered for 30 to 45 minutes, skimming off any foam that floats to the surface, until the pork is tender. Add the eggs (if using) and simmer for another 15 minutes before removing from the heat.
3 Serve hot with fresh vegetables and steamed rice.

Serves 4   Preparation time: 15 mins + 1 hour to marinate   Cooking time: 1 hour

Grilled Pork Meatballs   Nem Nuong

1 lb (500 g) ground pork
1/2 teaspoon salt
7 oz (200 g) pork fatback
2 tablespoons sugar
2 cloves garlic, minced
2 finger-length red chilies, deseeded
  and minced
1 teaspoon salt
3/4 tablespoon ground white pepper
12 bamboo skewers, soaked in water
  for 1 hour before using
2 tablespoons ground roasted unsalted peanuts (optional)
Fish Sauce Dip (page 26), for dipping

Accompaniments (optional)
1 cup (50 g) bean sprouts
1 starfruit, washed and thinly sliced
2 medium unripe bananas, peeled
  and thinly sliced
1/2 small cucumber, halved and
  thinly sliced

1 Combine the ground pork and salt in a bowl and mix well. Set aside.
2 Pan-fry the pork fatback in a skillet over medium heat for about 8 minutes. Remove and set aside to cool, then slice into very thin strips. Season the pork strips with the sugar, garlic, chilies, salt and pepper, and set aside for at least 5 minutes, then combine with the ground pork and mix well.
3 Wet your hands, spoon 1 heaping tablespoon of the pork mixture and shape it into a ball. Repeat until all the pork mixture is used up.
4 Thread the meatballs onto bamboo skewers. Grill the meatballs, a few skewers at a time, on a pan grill or under a preheated broiler using medium heat for about 5 minutes each, turning frequently, until cooked.
5 Sprinkle the grilled meatballs with ground peanuts (if using) and serve with the Accompaniments and a bowl of Fish Sauce Dip (page 26) on the side.

Makes 12 sticks   Preparation time: 30 mins   Cooking time: 15 mins

Grilled Pork Skewers with Rice Noodles   Bun Thit Nuong

1 lb (500 g) pork neck or shoulder,
  cubed
7 oz (200 g) dried string-like rice
  noodles (bun) or rice vermicelli
1 spring onion, green parts only,
  thinly sliced
15 bamboo skewers, soaked in water
  for 1 hour before using
Sprigs of Asian basil leaves,
  to garnish
2 cups Carrot and Radish Pickles
  (page 25), to serve (optional)
Peanut Sauce (page 26), for dipping

Marinade:
1 teaspoon minced garlic
2 baby leeks or spring onions, sliced
3 tablespoons fish sauce
1/2 teaspoon ground white pepper
1 tablespoon sugar

1 Combine the Marinade ingredients in a large bowl and mix well. Place the pork cubes in the Marinade and mix until well coated. Set aside to marinate for at least 20 minutes.
2 Bring a pot of water to a boil. Add the rice noodles and boil until soft, 5 to 7 minutes or longer as needed. Remove and rinse with cold water, then drain. Transfer to individual serving bowls and sprinkle the noodles with spring onion on top. Set aside.
3 Thread the marinated pork onto bamboo skewers. Grill the skewers, a few at a time, on a pan grill or under a preheated broiler using medium heat, turning and basting frequently with the Marinade, for about 5 minutes each, until the pork is cooked through and evenly browned on all sides.
4 Arrange the grilled pork skewers on a serving platter and garnish with basil leaves. Serve with the rice noodles, Carrot and Radish Pickles (if using) and a bowl of Peanut Sauce (page 26) on the side.

Makes 15 sticks   Preparation time: 30 mins   Cooking time: 10 mins

Grilled Beef Rolls Wrapped in Wild Betel Leaves   Bo La Lot

The Vietnamese are famous for their rolls and almost every dinner features at least two or three different types of rolls at the start of the meal.

1 lb (500 g) ground beef
5 oz (150 g) pork fatback
1 teaspoon sugar
1/4 teaspoon salt
20 large wild betel leaves (see note)
  or grape leaves, soaked in water to
  soften and drained
1 tablespoon oil, for grilling
Fish Sauce Dip (page 26), for dipping

Marinade
2 teaspoons five spice powder
2 teaspoons curry powder
1/2 teaspoon turmeric powder
2 teaspoons sugar
1 tablespoon soy sauce
2 tablespoons minced lemongrass
  (from inner part of the thick end of
  the stalk)
2 cloves garlic, minced
1 teaspoon ground white pepper

1 Combine the Marinade ingredients in a bowl and mix well. Pour the Marinade over the ground beef, mix until well blended and allow to marinate for at least 30 minutes.

2 In a skillet, pan-fry the pork fatback over medium heat for about 8 minutes. Remove and set aside to cool, then slice into very thin strips. Mix the pork strips with the sugar and salt, set aside for 15 minutes, then combine with the ground beef and mix well.

3 Place 1 heaping tablespoon of the mixture onto a betel leaf and roll the leaf up tightly, enclosing the filling. Thread the roll on a bamboo skewer. Continue to make the rolls in the same manner and thread about 3 rolls on each bamboo skewer. Repeat until all the ingredients are used up.

4 Brush each skewer with a little oil. Grill the skewered rolls on a pan grill or under a preheated broiler using medium heat for about 5 minutes on each side, until the betel leaves are slightly charred.

5 Serve the grilled rolls with a bowl of Fish Sauce Dip (page 26) on the side.

Note: You can also try adding fresh rice noodles into the wrap. Grape leaves may be substituted for the betel leaves. Use large leaves if possible, otherwise use 2 leaves together.

Serves 6   Preparation time: 25 mins   Cooking time: 10 mins

Fragrant Beef Stew   Bo Kho

This is the Vietnamese variation of a traditional French dish.

3 tablespoons oil
2 tablespoons annatto seeds
5 cloves garlic, minced
1 large onion, diced
2 tablespoons sugar
1 tablespoon salt
2 lbs (1 kg) top round (top-side) beef, cut into chunks
1 tablespoon curry powder
1 cup (250 ml) beer or water
1 stalk lemongrass, thick bottom part only, outer layers discarded, inner part
  bruised
3 star anise pods
1 cinnamon stick (3 in/8 cm)
1 carrot, sliced diagonally
1 lime, sliced, to serve
1 cup (40 g) mint leaves, to serve
Salt, Pepper and Lime Mix (page 27), to serve

1 Heat the oil in a wok or skillet over medium heat. Briefly stir-fry the annatto seeds until the oil turns reddish-brown. Remove from the heat, strain the oil and discard the seeds.
2 Combine $1/2$ of the annatto flavored oil, $1/2$ of the garlic, the onion, sugar and salt in a large bowl. Add the beef chunks and mix well. Allow to marinate for at least 30 minutes.
3 Heat the remaining annatto flavored oil over medium heat. Stir-fry the remaining garlic until fragrant and golden brown, 1 to 2 minutes. Add the curry powder, beer or water and marinated beef, and mix well. Bring the mixture to a boil, then add a little water, lemongrass, star anise and cinnamon, and stir well. Reduce the heat to low and braise the beef uncovered for about 45 minutes until tender. Add the carrot and simmer for another 10 minutes until cooked. Remove from the heat.
4 Serve the beef stew with lime, mint leaves and a bowl of Salt, Pepper and Lime Mix (page 27) on the side.

Note: You may wish to remove the star anise and cinnamon stick before serving. This dish can easily be refrigerated and reheated the next day, and tastes even better when the spices have had time to mingle.

Serves 6   Preparation time: 20 mins   Cooking time: 1 hour

Vietnamese Beef Hot Pot *Bo Nhung Dam*

This dish is traditionally served in a chafing dish, set in the middle of the table. Good fun, informal dining—everyone helps themselves.

1¹/₂ teaspoons sugar
1 teaspoon salt
1 teaspoon ground white pepper
2 lbs (1 kg) beef tenderloin, thinly sliced
Fermented Anchovy Dip (page 26), for dipping
20 dried rice paper wrappers (each 8 in/20 cm in diameter), dipped briefly in water to soften

Dip
1 cup (250 ml) vinegar
1 cup (250 ml) fresh coconut juice
2 medium onions, thinly sliced
3 tablespoons thinly sliced lemongrass (from inner part of the thick end of the stalk)
2 tablespoons Crispy Fried Shallots (page 42)
1 tablespoon sugar
¹/₂ teaspoon salt
¹/₄ teaspoon ground white pepper

Garnish
1 small cucumber, peeled and sliced
3 baby leeks or spring onions, minced
¹/₂ cup (50 g) ground roasted unsalted peanuts
1 cup (50 g) bean sprouts
1 small head butter lettuce, washed and separated
1 starfruit, washed and sliced
3 unripe bananas, peeled and sliced
7 oz (200 g) dried string-like rice noodles (*bun*) or rice vermicelli, boiled in water until softened

1 Rub the sugar, salt and pepper onto the beef slices. Allow to marinate for at least 15 minutes before serving.
2 Combine the Dip ingredients in a saucepan or small pot and bring to a boil over high heat, then transfer to a hot pot on the dining table and keep the Dip simmering. Arrange the beef, Fermented Anchovy Dip (page 26), rice paper wrappers and Garnish around the Dip.
3 Invite your guests to dip the beef slices very briefly in the hot Dip until just cooked. Remove and wrap the beef slices with various garnishes in the rice paper wrappers. Dip the wrapped beef in the Fermented Anchovy Dip (page 26) and eat immediately.

Note: The best method for cooking the beef is to use long chopsticks. Since the slices are so thin, they should require very brief moments in the Dip, unless you like the beef well done.

Serves 8 to 10   Preparation time: 30 mins

Husband and Wife Cakes   Banh Phu The

A traditional Vietnamese dessert from Hue, its name comes from the two parts that are tied together with a string of coconut and encased in a delicate box made of pandanus leaves.

4 cups (1 liter) water
5 cups (500 g) tapioca flour
1¹/₃ cups (250 g) sugar
¹/₂ cup (50 g) freshly grated coconut
²/₃ cup (150 g) dried yellow mung
  beans, soaked in water overnight
  to soften
¹/₂ cup (125 ml) sugar syrup (¹/₂ cup/
  100 g sugar dissolved in ¹/₂ cup/
  125 ml boiling water)
1 tablespoon oil
1 teaspoon fragrant essence (pomelo,
  pandanus or orange)
10 pandanus leaf cups (see note) or
  cup cake molds

1 Heat the water, tapioca flour, sugar and grated coconut in a saucepan or small pot over low heat for about 10 minutes, stirring constantly, until the mixture turns into a paste. Remove and set aside to cool.

2 Steam the soaked mung beans for about 20 minutes until cooked. Remove and mash into a paste. Combine with the sugar syrup and oil in a small pot and heat over low heat for about 10 minutes, stirring constantly, until the mixture is thick. Add the fragrant essence, mix well and remove from the heat.

3 Place a thin layer of the tapioca paste into each pandanus leaf cup or cup cake mold. Add 1 tablespoon of the mung bean paste on top and cover with another layer of the tapioca paste. Steam the cakes in a steamer for about 20 minutes, until transparent and cooked.

Note: To make a pandanus leaf cup, cut a pandanus leaf into 10 in (25 cm) long segments, with its ridge running along the center. On one side, snip the leaf until the center into 5 equal sections, each measuring 2 in (5 cm) long. Hold the leaf with the snipped side facing down, then fold in from one end of the leaf, overlapping the snipped sections as you fold, until a 2-in (5-cm) square cup is formed. Secure the end with a toothpick or staple.

Makes 10 cakes   Preparation time: 45 mins   Cooking time: 1 hour

Steamed Rice Flour and Mung Bean Cakes with Coconut Sauce
Banh Goi

1¹/₂ cups (200 g) rice flour
1¹/₃ cups (250 g) sugar
2¹/₂ cups (625 ml) pandanus juice, or
  1 teaspoon pandanus essence mixed
  with 2¹/₂ cups (625 ml) water
²/₃ cup (150 g) dried yellow mung
  beans, soaked in water overnight to
  soften
1 tablespoon vanilla essence
15 banana leaf pieces (each 8 x 6 in/
  20 x 15 cm), soaked in hot water to
  soften, for wrapping
2 tablespoons oil, for greasing the
  banana leaves
Toothpicks, for fastening
1¹/₂ cups (375 ml) thick coconut milk
3 tablespoons sugar
¹/₂ teaspoon salt
¹/₂ tablespoon cornstarch
2 tablespoons roasted sesame seeds

1 Combine the rice flour, ²/₃ cup (130 g) of the sugar and 2 cups (500 ml) of the pandanus juice in a saucepan. Heat over low heat, stirring constantly, until the mixture thickens to a paste, about 20 minutes. Remove from the heat.

2 Heat the soaked mung beans, remaining sugar and vanilla essence in a saucepan or small pot over low heat, stirring constantly, until the mixture thickens to a similar consistency as the rice flour paste, about 5 minutes. Remove and set aside to cool. Wet your hands and roll the mung bean paste into 15 small balls. Set aside.

3 Lightly grease a piece of the banana leaf with a little oil. Spread 1 tablespoon of the rice flour paste in the middle of the leaf and place a mung bean ball on top, then cover the mung bean ball with more rice flour paste. Fold one of the longer ends of the banana leaf over the filling, then the other longer side over it tightly. Tuck both sides of the leaf underneath and secure the packet with toothpicks. Repeat until all the ingredients are used up. Steam the rice cakes for about 20 minutes until cooked.

4 Heat the remaining pandanus juice, coconut milk, sugar, salt and cornstarch in a saucepan over medium heat, stirring occasionally, until the sugar is dissolved and the mixture is thick, about 10 minutes. Remove and transfer to a serving bowl.

5 To serve, unwrap the rice cakes. Sprinkle some sesame seeds on top and spread the coconut sauce over them.

Makes 15 cakes   Preparation time: 30 mins   Cooking time: 40 mins

Bananas and Sago Pearls in Coconut Cream   Che Chuoi Chung

6 small ripe bananas, peeled
3/4 cup (150 g) sugar
4 cups (1 liter) thin coconut milk
1/2 cup (75 g) sago pearls
2 pandanus leaves
1 cup (250 ml) thick coconut milk
Ground roasted unsalted peanuts or
  sesame seeds, to serve

1 Sprinkle the bananas with the sugar and set aside.
2 In a saucepan, heat the thin coconut milk, sago and pandanus leaves over medium heat for about 15 minutes, stirring occasionally. Add the bananas and simmer for about 5 minutes, then add the thick coconut milk, mix well and remove from the heat.
3 Serve in individual serving bowls, sprinkled with ground peanuts or sesame seeds on top.

Serves 4   Preparation time: 15 mins   Cooking time: 20 mins

Slush Ice Lychee in Coconut Milk

1/2 can canned longan
1/2 can canned lychee
3 tablespoons sago pearls
2 cups (500 ml) water
Crushed ice
1/2 cup (125 ml) thick coconut milk,
  chilled
4 tablespoons condensed milk
Sprigs of mint leaves, to garnish

1 Drain the longan and lychee, and reserve the syrup. Set aside.
2 In a saucepan, bring the sago and water to a boil, then reduce the heat to medium and simmer for about 15 minutes, stirring constantly, until the sago turns transparent. Remove from the heat and rinse with cold water, then drain. Set aside.
3 To serve, place 1 heaping tablespoon of the cooked sago in a tall serving glass, followed by some crushed ice, 2 tablespoons of the coconut milk, another heaping tablespoon of the sago, some lychee and longan. Drizzle 2 tablespoons of the fruit syrup and 1 tablespoon of the condensed milk on top and garnish with mint leaves.

Serves 4   Preparation time: 10 mins   Cooking time: 15 mins

Pineapple Tartlets   Banh Nuong Nhan Thom

24 tartlet molds (each 2 in/5 cm in
   diameter)

Dough
1 cup (225 g) soft salted butter
$1/4$ cup (50 g) sugar
$1/2$ cup (125 ml) fresh milk
4 cups (600 g) flour
2 eggs, beaten

Filling
1 large or 2 small pineapples (about
   3 lbs/$1 1/4$ kg in total) peeled, cored,
   minced or chopped in a food
   processor
1 cup (200 g) sugar
2 drops vanilla essence

1 Make the Dough first by combining the butter, sugar and milk in a mixing bowl and beating until well blended. Fold in the flour and continue beating until a smooth dough is formed. Flour your hands and using a rolling pin, roll the Dough on a floured surface to $1/8$ in (3 mm) thick. Cut out circles large enough to line the tartlet molds. Lightly flour each mold and line with a Dough circle. Cut the remaining Dough into thin strips.
2 Preheat the oven to 300°F (150°C).
3 To make the Filling, heat the pineapple and sugar in a saucepan over low heat for about 45 minutes, stirring continuously, until the mixture is thickened. Add the vanilla essence, mix well and remove from the heat.
4 Fill each mold with the Filling and lay the Dough strips to form a criss-cross pattern on top. Brush with the beaten egg and bake in the oven for 30 minutes until golden brown.

Makes 24 tartlets   Preparation time: 35 mins   Cooking time: 1 hour 10 mins

Quick Banana Coconut Cake   Banh Chuoi Nuong

$1 3/4$ lbs (800 g) ripe bananas (about
   5 bananas), peeled and thinly
   sliced lengthwise
1 cup (200 g) sugar
$3/4$ cup (185 ml) coconut cream
$1/2$ teaspoon vanilla essence
8 slices sandwich bread
2 tablespoons melted butter
Vanilla ice cream, to serve (optional)

1 Sprinkle the banana slices with $1/2$ of the sugar.
2 In a small pot, heat the remaining sugar and coconut cream over medium heat until the sugar is dissolved. Add the vanilla essence and mix well. Remove from the heat.
3 Remove and discard the crusts from the bread. Briefly soak the bread in the sweetened coconut cream and transfer to a plate. Set aside.
4 Preheat the oven to 350°F (180°C).
5 Grease a cake pan (12 in/30 cm in diameter) with some butter. Arrange a layer of the banana slices on the base of the pan, then top with a layer of the bread. Repeat to lay alternate layers of banana and bread in the pan and finish the top layer with the banana slices. Drizzle the remaining butter over the top. Cover with aluminium foil and bake in the oven for about 1 hour. Remove from the heat and set aside for 12 hours before slicing.
6 Serve the banana cake with vanilla ice cream (if using).

Serves 4   Preparation time: 15 mins   Cooking time: 1 hour 15 mins

Measurements and conversions

Measurements in this book are given in volume as far as possible. Teaspoon, tablespoon and cup measurements should be level, not heaped, unless otherwise indicated. Australian readers please note that the standard Australian measuring spoon is larger than the UK or American spoon by 5 ml, so use $^3/_4$ tablespoon instead of a full tablespoon when following the recipes.

Liquid Conversions

Imperial	Metric	US cups
$^1/_2$ fl oz	15 ml	1 tablespoon
1 fl oz	30 ml	$^1/_8$ cup
2 fl oz	60 ml	$^1/_4$ cup
3 fl oz	85 ml	$^1/_3$ cup
4 fl oz	125 ml	$^1/_2$ cup
5 fl oz	150 ml	$^2/_3$ cup
6 fl oz	175 ml	$^3/_4$ cup
8 fl oz	250 ml	1 cup
12 fl oz	375 ml	$1^1/_2$ cups
16 fl oz	500 ml	2 cups
	1 liter	4 cups

Note:
1 UK pint = 20 fl oz
1 US pint = 16 fl oz

Solid Weight Conversions

Imperial	Metric
$^1/_2$ oz	15 g
1 oz	28 g
$1^1/_2$ oz	45 g
2 oz	60 g
3 oz	85 g
$3^1/_2$ oz	100 g
4 oz ($^1/_4$ lb)	125 g
5 oz	150 g
6 oz	175 g
7 oz	200 g
8 oz ($^1/_2$ lb)	225 g
9 oz	260 g
10 oz	300 g
16 oz (1 lb)	450 g
32 oz (2 lbs)	1 kg

Oven Temperatures

Heat	Fahrenheit	Centigrade/Celsius	British Gas Mark
Very cool	230	110	$^1/_4$
Cool or slow	275–300	135–150	1–2
Moderate	350	175	4
Hot	425	220	7
Very hot	450	230	8

Index of Recipes

Mail-order/online sources

The ingredients used in this book can all be found in markets featuring the foods of Southeast Asia. Many of them can also be found in any well-stocked supermarket or Korean specialty store. Ingredients not found locally may be available from the mail-order and online sources listed below.

AsianWok.com
www.asianwok.com

Anzen Importers
736 NE Union Avenue
Portland, OR 97232
Tel: 503-233-5111

Central Market
40th and North Lamar
Austin, TX 78756
Tel: 512-206-1000
www.centralmarket.com

Dekalb World Farmers Market
3000 East Ponce De Leon
Decatur, GA 30034
Tel: 404-377-6401
www.dekalbfarmersmarket.com

Dean & Deluca
560 Broadway (Prince St)
New York, NY 10012
Tel: 212-226-800
www.deandeluca.com

EthnicGrocer.com
www.ethnicgrocer.com

Gourmail, Inc.
816 Newton Road
Berwyn, PA 19312
Tel: 215-296-4620

HanAhReum Asian Mart
1720 Route 70 E.
Cherry Hill, NJ 08003
Tel: 856-489-4611
www.hanahreum.com
(Korean language website)

ikoreaplaza.com
www.ikoreaplaza.com

Kam Man Food Products
219 Quincy Avenue
Quincy, MA 02169-6754
Tel: 212-755-3566
www.kammanfood.net

KoaMart
www.koamart.com

Nancy's Specialty Market
P.O. Box 327
Wye Mills, MD 21679
Tel: 800-462-6291

Oriental Food Market and Cooking School
2801 Howard Street
Chicago, IL 60645
Tel: 312-274-2826

Oriental Market
502 Pampas Drive
Austin, TX 78752
Tel: 512-453-9058

Pacific Mercantile Company, Inc.
1925 Lawrence Street
Denver, CO 80202
Tel: 303-295-0293
www.pacificmercantile.com

Uwajimaya
600 5th Ave South, Suite 100
Seattle, WA 98104
Tel: 206-624-6248
www.uwajimaya.com

Wasabi
10194 SW Parkway
Portland, OR
Tel: 503-292-1861